Games Teaching

An Approach for the Primary School

Games Teaching
An Approach for the Primary School

E. Mauldon, M.A.,
Formerly Deputy Principal, Lady Mabel College of Education

H.B. Redfern, Ph.D., M.Ed.,
Free-lance lecturer in Philosophy of Education and Aesthetics

MACDONALD AND EVANS

Macdonald & Evans Ltd
Estover, Plymouth PL6 7PZ

First published 1969
Reprinted 1970
Reprinted 1972
Reprinted 1976
Second edition 1981

© Macdonald & Evans Ltd 1981

ISBN: 0 7121 0739 8

Printed in Great Britain by
J.W. Arrowsmith Ltd, Bristol

Preface to the Second Edition

This book, first published in 1969, was originally prompted by our uneasiness about the teaching of school games in general and about the procedures commonly in use at the Primary level in particular. In the Preface to that edition we claimed that "as soon as one begins to review the assumptions underlying both the content and manner of most Games teaching, it becomes obvious that fresh thinking in this field is long overdue. The aims as commonly stated are educationally suspect, the methods out of step with current thought and practice . . . ."

Twelve years later we still find cause for the same disquiet, although the need of which we then spoke for a critical reappraisal of the contribution, if any, which games might be thought to make to a general education has, to some extent, been recognised — even if chiefly by writers outside the sphere of physical education rather than by those within. The preparation of a second edition has therefore been undertaken in the hope that this recognition will become more widespread, that at least some of the literature (especially by philosophers) on competition and on games in education that has been published in recent years will become increasingly familiar to teachers, and that more and more practitioners will be prepared to consider and adopt, as some have done already, the sort of approach we advocate to games teaching not only in Primary and Middle schools but also at the lower Secondary stage as well.

Although progress has been disappointingly slow, a number of factors are currently at work that would seem likely to accelerate the changes in thought and practice we continue to believe are desirable. One such factor concerns developing courses in the education and training of teachers. For in Institutions of Higher Education even greater stress than previously is now laid on the importance of independent and critical thinking on the part of students and of their being prepared to question intelligently the beliefs and attitudes that govern educational practice as a whole and in particular subjects. Courses in physical education for intending teachers, no less than others, have been obliged to undergo re-examination and often re-structuring in order to give greater consideration to fundamental questions about the nature of the knowledge and skill involved, specific objectives, and appropriate means of evaluation. Thus many games courses, which in the past consisted of little more than personal participation in, for example, football, hockey, cricket, tennis and netball, together with instruction in how to teach these activities, are being replaced by more broadly-based schemes with increased conceptual content and concerned with general principles rather than with the acquisition of a narrow range of highly-specialised techniques.

Young teachers in particular, and those who have pursued further studies in Education and/or Physical Education, might therefore be expected to find this book more immediately relevant, as well as more practically useful, than the usual textbooks on the subject. For these are apt to dodge the vital issues inevitably raised by the whole notion of competitive games as an educational enterprise and to take for granted just those convictions and values that tend to underpin the teaching of the subject, but that we have long been of the opinion should be vigorously challenged. However, our observations and suggestions are addressed also to any teacher who is aware of the questionable foundations upon which much games teaching rests and who may be disturbed by the generally unsatisfactory state of affairs in respect of games in schools, especially at the Primary level.

Lack of personal prowess or of knowledge about the rules

and techniques of particular games need not, we argue, prevent teachers with a sound grasp of educational principles
and an understanding of children's development and various
ways of learning from using profitably the time set aside for
games, at least with younger age-groups; while those in charge
of older pupils should be able to make use of our recommendations to supplement their existing programmes and adapt
their methods as they find appropriate. Specialists and semi-
specialists who are, or who have been, games players themselves will, we hope, be able to draw on the material offered
in these pages in order to use their expertise to the best advantage and relate it to educational issues.

This, then, is not a coaching manual, although references
to some of the major games and to certain skills are made in
some detail in Chapters 4 and 6. Instead, it provides an analysis and classification of a wide range of games, so making possible, we suggest, a more comprehensive understanding of
such activities and the invention of new varieties. It remains
only to define, for the limited purpose of this book, what we
mean by the word "game" — a term that can be used to cover
an almost infinite variety of pursuits but which requires restriction in the context of physical education. Here we take
it initially to denote *an activity in which a minimum of two
people, themselves on the move, engage in competitive play
with a moving object within the framework of certain rules.*

March, 1981   H.B.R.
                                                                              E.M.

Acknowledgments to the Second Edition

We remain indebted to the following for their assistance in connection with those parts of the original text that have been incorporated in this second edition:

Mrs Howlett (formerly Mrs Pain), for help in carrying out some of the experimental work with children, and Mr Bishop who kindly provided classes for this purpose;

Mrs Marian Clarke, and Mr Stubbs and members of his staff, for similar assistance; and the many friends and colleagues who read and discussed with us the original text, in particular Dr Ida Webb and Mr Eric Ward, for their advice in respect of Chapter 6.

March, 1981

H.B.R.
E.M.

Contents

CHAPTER 1

Games in Education

A major topic in educational discussion during recent years *Good* has been the content of the school curriculum. Questions as *for* to whether there should be a so-called core curriculum, com- *timed* pulsory for all pupils and surrounded by a cluster of optional *essay* subjects,[1] together with allied questions as to which subjects are to be assigned to which category, have provoked consider-able debate among both those "inside" and those "outside" education.

Clearly, there can be little of more fundamental importance for teachers, as well as for others within a liberal democracy, to consider; and such questions, along with those to do with the justification of a particular subject as a curriculum activity, what its objectives might be thought to be, how it is to be assessed, and so on, will no doubt continue to exercise the minds of thoughtful practitioners and theorists alike for some time to come. For not only *education,* but also a number of concepts that arise in connection with it (e.g. democracy, competition, art, history), would seem precisely of the kind that Gallie has illuminatingly suggested are "essentially com-plex and essentially contested".[2]

Within such debate, as well as in practice, the subject of physical education (if it *can* count as a "subject") occupies a peculiarly ambivalent position. On the one hand, it has been by tradition — in striking contrast, it may be noted, to what obtains in most Continental countries, both Western and

1

Eastern — a feature of the compulsory curriculum; indeed it is not long ago, relatively speaking, that this was one of the few subjects which (though for dubious educational reasons) every teacher was required to take during his or her initial training. On the other hand, it has remained until recent times comparatively undiscussed by those outside its own ranks, and the case for some form of compulsory physical education on specifically educational grounds — which its title warrants if it is not to be an empty or merely pretentious phrase — has not yet been successfully made out. Nor is it likely that it could be, given the number of widely-assorted pursuits that are now included within it; rather, its various branches demand separate consideration from this point of view.

Foremost among those pursuits requiring critical scrutiny, we believe, is games. For this type of activity — games, that is, as defined in the Preface to this book — has always held a central place within physical education, and long before that hazy notion ever emerged was widely accepted as an integral feature of the common curriculum. In fact in some — perhaps especially boys' — schools games have *constituted* "physical education". Even today, when a range of options in this sphere may be open to pupils at the Secondary stage, a vast proportion will typically be found to be competitive games. As for children in Primary and Middle schools, no choice whatsoever may be expected in this matter: participation in games is usually assumed unquestioningly to be an essential ingredient of the staple diet. Indeed, it seems almost un-British to suggest that education could be complete without them.

Yet of all the kinds of activity which fall under the heading "physical education" this probably is the one most difficult to justify as an educational enterprise. Worse yet, the idea of playing games compulsorily can be shown both to contain a logically absurd element and to be morally objectionable. In order to understand this it is necessary to consider in more detail the character of the sort of games here under discussion — that is, games of the competitive variety, as contrasted with, say, singing games, games of chance, make-believe, imitation, and so on.[3] In the first place, although with several forms of play it may be difficult to draw a hard and fast line

between what is "serious" and what is "non-serious", what
is "real" and what "non-real", a game is in an important sense
set apart from the actual business of everyday life: it is as
Huizinga has put it, ". . . time-bound . . . it has no contact
with any reality outside itself, and its performance is its own
end."[4]

The framework of rules within which players compete is
thus, as Caillois (in his well-known classification of games)[5]
has pointed out, one that is artificially created; the rules of a
game are of a purely functional and arbitrary kind, having no
force or application beyond that specially invented situation.
They may, it is true, derive from what might be thought to
be fundamental moral principles such as fairness and justice;
on the other hand it is perfectly possible for one's moral
standards to conflict with what is permitted by the rules of
a game.[6] What is legitimate in, for example, contact games,
in which violence may be employed and consequently harm
perhaps inflicted on another's person (in at least one sense of
that somewhat curious term) may be deeply offensive to
many people's ethical sensibilities. Indeed for some, participating in or encouraging any activity in which striving to win
is a basic feature is morally abhorrent.

What the precise relationship is between rules in games and
moral rules and principles of everyday life is a complex aspect
of what is itself a complex and highly controversial matter,
namely how morality — and hence moral education — is to be
characterised. It is, of course, beyond the scope of a book
such as this to deal with this question in the depth it deserves.
Nevertheless, it seems clear that games are not entirely divorced from daily life — the world outside the "world" of the
game — inasmuch as if someone chooses to engage in such a
pursuit he enters, even if tacitly, into certain transactions
and agreements with others no less (though no more) than in
the case of any other type of interpersonal enterprise.[7] He
promises, in effect, to abide by certain rules — presumably in
order to enjoy the benefits, challenges, excitements, glories
(and disappointments?) that he sees as characteristic of the
game in question. Although he is not usually called upon to
give any verbal undertaking of a formal or overt kind, his very

participation and abiding by the rules is normally evidence of his having understood and freely consented to what is involved. *Normally,* we said. For an exception obviously arises when an individual is *compelled* to take part in a game — as is the case in many schools.

Such a situation is thus of a contradictory character, as well as being morally reprehensible. For the very notion of promising implies freedom and willingness, so that to be forced into "promising" to observe this or that set of rules means that what one then does is inevitably different from what one is supposed to be doing: in this instance one could hardly be said to be *playing a game* at all; and to oblige anyone to consent is morally objectionable since he is thereby obliged to act in bad faith, to participate against his will in something that of its nature presupposes entering into certain commitments freely. It would seem, then, that on any but a grotesque view of education compulsory games not only lack educational value altogether but can be positively *anti*-educative.

Even if participation is voluntary, however, the essentially competitive nature of games raises serious questions about their place in education. For what is central to such activities is the intention to win — to win, moreover, in a way that is clearly demonstrable to everyone. Teachers (and others) might try to play down the importance of winning — or losing — but to suggest to participants that they should play so as *not* to win would be to make nonsense of the entire undertaking. No matter what the spirit in which a match may be played on a particular occasion, it is an indispensable feature of a game that one individual or side sets out to score over another: to try to do otherwise would be to engage in something else. All the moves a player makes — including, it may be noted, the deliberate breaking or subtle flouting of the rules — make sense only on the presupposition that he is endeavouring to beat someone; and every game, however different from others in respect of equipment, manoeuvres, methods of play and scoring, and so forth, shares this feature with the rest.

Here we find an important contrast with other activities usually included in the physical education programme of schools (the other exception is athletics, though even in this case it is possible in most events to seek merely to better one's own record). Gymnastics, dancing,[8] swimming, canoeing, rock-climbing, and so forth, can (like acting, singing, rose-growing, dress-making, and a great many other pursuits) be *made* competitive, but this is not one of their defining characteristics: they retain their point and remain recognisably dancing, canoeing, singing, etc., when *no* competition is involved.

Despite, however, the increasing concern that has been voiced in recent years about competition in general and to a certain extent about competitive games in particular in education, many teachers with responsibility for physical education seem to remain singularly complacent in this matter and apparently unprepared to examine critically either the nature of the games they teach or the assumptions on which beliefs about their proclaimed values typically rest. Moreover, those who do attempt to take up the challenges posed by enquirers into the claims put forward on behalf of games for a place in the school curriculum usually seek refuge in arguments whose flimsiness and implausibility may easily be exposed by anyone with even a modest amount of philosophical or psychological understanding. The most frequently quoted reasons have to do principally with moral issues (the supposed usefulness of games as regards what are thought to be man's innate competitiveness and aggression and their alleged socialising and character-building virtues); so-called leisure education; the need for compensation for mental activity; exercise and health; and enjoyment and relief from tension.

None of these claims as they are usually formulated, however, stands up to examination. Talk, for instance, about competitiveness and aggression being "natural" or "innate" in human beings raises complex, but in most cases insufficiently appreciated problems as to what these terms mean and how such statements could ever be verified. The possibility that these traits might be socially developed, along with the fact that, even in societies in which competition plays a major role in life generally, there are individuals and groups who operate in quite contrary ways, seems often to be overlooked by proponents of competitive activities. Perhaps this simply indicates a failure of insight and awareness on the part of many games enthusiasts (among others): as Bailey has noted, "highly competitive people seem to find it very difficult to imagine or understand those who are not."[9] But in any case, even if proof were forthcoming as to which, if any, characteristics are inborn and which acquired, this would supply no ready solution to questions involving decision-making, such as those concerned with curriculum content: whether particular tendencies are to be fostered or inhibited and controlled is a matter for discussion about what is thought to be desirable, not merely possible or perhaps easily developed. And the claim that games provide socially acceptable and safe channels for the re-directing of competitive urges immediately invites the objection that, judging by the behaviour both on and off the scene of play of many professional *and* non-professional players (not to mention their "fans"), there is just as much likelihood that these urges are intensified and aggravated by playing (or even watching) games as that they are harmlessly siphoned off or held in check.

If, alternatively, it is suggested that school games provide a means whereby young people can become equipped to enter and hold their own in a competitive world, the claim falls down on at least two counts: first, it assumes some straightforward carry-over from the playing-field to everyday life, and secondly, it makes no allowance for the view that, rather than prepare youngsters to accommodate to society as it is, education should help them to regard its values critically and perhaps seek to change some of them.

Any attempt to justify games in terms of moral education should, furthermore, recognise that since what is involved is a specially contrived situation, the whole notion of a game logically presupposes some grasp of what it is to be fair, honest, equal before the "law", and so forth. This is not to say that in practice — with young children especially — such concepts may not be re-inforced, or even possibly acquired, through the experience of games; but in the main participation in a game *re*flects rather than *af*fects an individual's understanding of and attitudes towards certain moral principles and codes of conduct. In other words, it is more typically an occasion for exercising and manifesting the moral sensibilities he already has (as well as for demonstrating those he lacks). As Bailey puts it:

> Competitive games . . . are dramatic evidence of the state of moral education and moral development of their players and spectators . . . . We cannot hope to improve moral education by playing more football, but we might help people to play football more morally by improving moral education.[10]

Allied claims about games being of educational value in virtue of the character-building qualities and interpersonal relationships they are said to foster fare even worse: such claims would have, once more, to rest either on a conception (or rather, misconception) of a game as a slice of actual life, lacking that set-apart character which is part of what makes a game what it is ("only a game"); or on a misplaced confidence in the possibility of a transference of training of the kind that has long since been discredited. Unhappily, the suggestion that games are always played in a spirit of goodwill, courtesy, friendliness, and the like, is hardly borne out by the evidence all around us: even so-called friendly matches merit the title no more than the other (unfriendly?) variety. There are, then, no grounds for the widely-held nineteenth-century beliefs that fair play on the sports field promotes just dealing off it; that "team spirit" develops a general ability and inclination to co-operate with others in a variety of walks of life; or that losing gracefully in games leads to chivalrous behaviour in everyday situations. As Aspin remarks:

> The idea that "the battle of Waterloo was won on the playing fields of Eton" belongs more to the repertory of folklore, ideology or mysticism than to any sensible view of the function of education.[11]

It is in any case a matter for debate whether some of the character traits frequently held in such high esteem by those who preach the gospel of team games *are* wholly admirable; and it is not surprising that for some time now many young people have rejected outright the image, typically associated with the playing of such games, of toughness, heartiness and unquestioned loyalty to a particular group — especially to one not of their own choosing or devoted to an end that they may see as trivial or worthless.

This brings us to a consideration of the claim that one of the values of games lies in the contribution they make to "leisure education". For there is ample evidence to show that the majority of school-leavers not only never go on to play team games themselves, but do not participate in any kind of game at all (although they may follow some sport as spectators).[12] Moreover, many who do take an active part in some sort of physical pursuit choose something other than those activities to which they have been introduced in schools.[13] Nor is this surprising, since such forms of recreation are often largely matters of fashion and apt to be as unpredictable and unstable as styles of dress or hair. Thus, in an age in which there is a constant proliferation of physical activities (some, such as skateboarding, of meteor-like appearance and transience), it would seem unlikely, even if it were desirable, that anyone could know what might be available, let alone popular, by the time any particular generation of schoolchildren were adult. It would not have been easy to predict, for example, the recent upsurge of interest in this country of water-sports, yoga, or the various forms of martial arts.

Of more serious and fundamental importance for educators, however, is the whole question of the relationship between education and leisure; or, more accurately, the notion of "leisure education". Once more, this is too vast a subject to pursue in any detail here; but it must be remarked that the very term has a strange ring. For an education that does not enable an individual to make profitable and enjoyable use of his spare time is scarcely worthy of the name. Far from leisure presenting him with a problem, anyone who has been educated (other than in the strictly limited sense of having merely passed through a system of schooling) does not require something *extra* in order to avoid boredom or inactivity during his leisure hours; rather, he will rarely have sufficient time to pursue the various avenues of skill and enquiry that his education will have either opened up to him directly or equipped him to become aware of to the extent that he has plenty to investigate later. *Any* school subject, therefore, might be said to have leisure value. But it does not, of course, follow that everything that might become a leisure activity in the future is of specifically educational importance for children during the time they are at school; and it is in *these* terms that games, like any other contender for a place in the curriculum, have to be justified.

As for the venerable idea that games serve as a compensation for mental activity, a makeweight for academic studies, or a useful expedient for the purpose of "letting off steam", this could hardly be thought to constitute a case for such activities, for at best it would mean that they are a means of *facilitating* education, rather than having educational merit in their own right. If they are to be thus regarded as having *value-by-contrast*,[14] then it has to be conceded that a great many other pursuits qualify equally well in this respect. A more basic difficulty, however, once again concerns meaning and the conceptual appropriateness of talk about mental activity *as opposed to* physical activity, mind *as opposed to* body, and so on. Furthermore, as far as Primary school children in particular are concerned, the days when there was a need for regular breaks from sedentary lessons have largely gone; contemporary methods of teaching, with their stress on an active exploration and use of the environment, usually ensure that there is considerable freedom of movement not only within the classroom and between various parts of the school building, but outside it as well.

The question arises here, however, as to how far the games traditionally taught in schools do satisfy the bodily needs of children. Until a reasonable degree of competence in the necessary skills has been acquired, most of these games not only fail to increase their powers of endurance, stamina and so forth, but actually restrict energetic activity — as witness the pathetic sight of shivering or immobile figures dotted about many a cricket pitch or netball court, or alternatively, even on a warm day, the capering and twirling around that have nothing to do with the game itself but in which children are apt to indulge when, as frequently happens, they are not within the vicinity of the ball. An extended mid-session break would often achieve far more in this respect. Indeed, the value of games in terms of physical exercise and health tends generally to be overrated. As a means of promoting all-round physical development they do not compare favourably with, for example, swimming or many forms of dance; and if the idea of a "breath of fresh air" is invoked in this connection, it might be pointed out that this is often achieved incidentally during the teaching of other areas of the curriculum such as science, art or environmental studies. In any case, this could hardly be thought to rank as an educational consideration as such.

This applies also to the question of enjoyment, claims about which are nevertheless still apt to be advanced in respect of games with monotonous regularity in spite of the avowed dislike expressed by at least a good many older children. Certainly it is part of a teacher's job to attempt to bring pupils to a discovery of the particular pleasures and satisfactions that belong to whatever type of understanding, skill or appreciation he is dealing with. It might also be the case that if someone enjoys what he is doing he learns it more easily or more quickly (though it is not impossible for successful learning to occur in the face of tedium, difficulty or frustration). But as regards the justification of a subject it is *what* an individual is trying to learn that has to be considered, not merely whether it is enjoyable for him or not. Clearly, it will not do to say either that what he does not enjoy is educationally worthless or that whatever he does enjoy is educationally important: it might, on the contrary, be trivial, harmful or destructive.

Claims about enjoyment are often coupled with claims about games providing relief from emotional and nervous tension (built up, it often seems to be assumed, by academic subjects). But while this might well be so in the case of some children, for others (especially the non-athletic, the non-aggressive and the non-competitive), the games lesson itself frequently creates new anxieties and new stresses. Those with little ability in or aptitude for games, for example, often suffer not only the mortification of constantly revealing their that anything has been heard of, for example, backwardness or "slow learners" in games, while giftedness in such activities has been apt to be looked upon as some sort of compensation for lack of intellectual ability. Some teachers, indeed, admit openly to regarding games as a waste of time and effort, or, at best, a luxury for which time in school hours is only grudgingly spared. If, of course, the objection is to compulsory games on genuinely moral grounds, this is entirely laudable. But many teachers in effect abdicate from the responsibility of rigorously thinking through their position on games and of finding out about the capabilities of the children in their charge in this sphere. Some class teachers often seem content either to ignore timetable provision for games or else to hand over their pupils to a colleague who is a games enthusiast or to one who is prepared to teach the one or two he knows, whatever these may be. The children may thus be left either to the expert — who all too often seeks to pass on his know-how without reflecting carefully and critically on the educational objectives of the enterprise or the suitability of his methods for the group in question — or to the apathetic or self-styled ignorant teacher who feels that he cannot cope with this aspect of the curriculum because he is not himself skilled in any of the major games and does not know the various rules.

Yet rather than having to be acquainted with particular games and details of their rules and specific techniques, Primary school teachers would do better, in our view, if they were to approach games teaching completely afresh, recognising how narrow is the interpretation usually placed on the word "game" by adults for purposes of education, and how consequently impoverished their imagination in the choice of activities selected for inclusion in the curriculum under that heading. A grasp of certain broad principles which we go on to suggest are common to all ball games (and allied varieties played with quoits and shuttles), together with their professional knowledge of children and of appropriate ways of learning at various stages, should, we believe, enable most teachers to make adequate provision for pupils at least up to nine or ten years of age, and in some cases beyond. For not all children,

deficiencies in a manner more public than is usually the case with non-physical activities, but also the humiliations and miseries of being exhorted to "play up", not to let the side down, and so on. The situation is often further exacerbated by those teachers who, in their haste to encourage competitive play and to promote representative sides, demand of children far too soon that they master specific and often difficult techniques. And in addition to the kind of frustration born of failure there may also be that engendered by boredom, particularly in cases where the many are neglected in favour of the few who have special aptitude, or where there is a lack of scope for exploration, discovery, invention and problem-solving (such as is characteristic of much games teaching). If to this it is objected that such frustrations could be prevented by improved methods of teaching, it might be replied that this applies equally to any subject: academic studies do not necessarily generate tension and misery, neither are games (or, for that matter, any other branch of physical education) a specially privileged means of lessening it. Such considerations belong anyway rather to the sphere of therapy than strictly to education.

It will be evident from the foregoing that we view *compulsory* games in schools as utterly indefensible; and precisely on what grounds games are best justified as an optional curriculum activity we have to confess is far from clear to us. Arguments to do with their possible contribution to some aspects of moral and/or aesthetic education, for example, seem too readily countered by the objections that such a contribution can only be incidental and therefore limited, and that moral and aesthetic education can be tackled more directly and effectively by other means.

Nevertheless, in a society in which, for better or worse, games play an important part in the lives of many people, either as participants or spectators, it might seem desirable that children should learn something *about* such activities, and perhaps have the chance to savour certain aspects at first hand, so that they can then make an informed decision as to whether or not to take part in fully competitive games if offered the chance. Without some direct, even if limited, experience of what is involved it is doubtful whether they could ever come to appreciate why some individuals find them worthwhile, or to think critically about the conduct and values associated with them. And since games are at present so strongly entrenched in the British system of education, we wish to offer teachers by way of immediate assistance some guidance as to how to utilise those periods on the timetable set aside for the purpose.

Moreover, at the Primary and early Secondary stages the situation tends to be somewhat less problematic inasmuch as games activities, in a wider sense of the term than that so far employed, have considerable appeal for many children (largely, perhaps, on account of the often unpredictable character of play involving moving objects and players on the move). It therefore seems worth considering whether, just as a widespread interest among children in gymnastic- and dance-like activities can be harnessed and developed for educational purposes, so too might an interest in play with balls, quoits, bats and such like — play that is not, however, necessarily competitive, but which can afford opportunities for acquiring skill and understanding in addition to being a source of fun and excitement.

But if such activities are to be taken seriously as having educative potential, it is essential that both among teachers and among those responsible for their training and further assistance there should be radical changes in thought and practice. For it is a curious but deplorable feature of the present situation that thinking about games, as well as the methods by which they are taught, is in the main completely at variance with the beliefs and procedures that are characteristic of the Primary school curriculum as a whole. Official pronouncements on the subject rarely, if ever, get to grips with this anomaly, let alone open up fresh lines of inquiry: indeed, they are apt to suffer from the same complacency and to be riddled with the same assumptions as those to which criticism has already been directed. Similarly, courses for teachers almost invariably concentrate on methods of coaching a narrow range of specific techniques belonging to the major team

games; although there might seem to be new "ideas", these in fact usually turn out to be based on stereotyped ways of approaching the subject of games so that it remains shut off from general educational considerations. Fundamental issues to do with the circumstances in which the teaching of games might be defensible, what should be the overall aims of such teaching at the Primary school level, what sort of lesson content and methods are suitable in the light of children's various stages of development and ways of learning, how individual differences and preferences might be catered for, and so forth, are rarely given the attention they deserve.

It is thus that, except in a comparatively few cases, a severely limited diet of ready-made adult games, or watered-down versions of these, is regularly served up to children under eleven, with little or no account taken, it would seem, of the degree of cognitive, social and moral maturity that such activities require, or of young children's difficulties in understanding rules and co-operating with others for the purpose of outwitting opponents. What govern most school programmes would seem to be merely national, local and school traditions, or simply the personal preferences of an individual teacher. Little attention appears to be paid to the decline in popularity among most young people during the last two decades of single-sex and team games (the trend has been consistently towards activities which cater for small numbers and in which the sexes can participate together); and although some of those who do continue to play games after their school days are over claim that what they value is the challenge of the activity itself, the majority would probably agree that the social aspect is at least of equal importance. Yet even in the Primary school the sexes are often completely separated for games, and neither boys nor girls given opportunities to become familiar with, say, shuttles or rackets of various kinds.

Moreover, in spite of the lip-service that is commonly paid to games, and the prevalence of attitudes of the kind discussed earlier, a child's achievements or failures in this sphere seem to be of little genuine concern to teachers in their assessment of his general educational progress. It is only very recently

it must be emphasised again, may wish to go on to participate in a fully competitive situation, and those who do not might more profitably do something entirely different or perhaps study, say, the history of certain games or games played in schools in other countries, or compare newspaper reports of matches or write their own accounts, and so on. They might also, of course, continue with experiments and problems of the kind we suggest in Chapter 9, possibly devising new ones both for themselves and for others.

In what follows we proceed, first, to examine in some detail what is involved in games of the kind that conform to the definition originally proposed, setting such activities in the context of young children's movement play in general, and relating them to the characteristics and stages of development at the Primary level that have particular relevance in this connection. This will enable us to recommend certain principles which we believe should govern the planning of games lessons at this stage — and perhaps beyond — and to make concrete suggestions as to how these may be implemented. But we wish to stress that the onus remains on teachers who have responsibility in this area to give more stringent thought, both individually and collectively, to the subject of games in school and to work out further courses of action that serve *educational* ends.

Notes

1. *See*, for example, White, J.P., *Towards a Compulsory Curriculum* (Routledge & Kegan Paul, 1973).
2. Gallie, W.B., "Essentially Contested Concepts", *Proceedings of the Aristotelian Society*, Vol. LVI (1956). On education as an "essentially contested concept", *see* Hartnett, A. & Naish, M. (eds.), *Theory and the Practice of Education*, Vol. I (Heinemann, 1976); similarly, on competition, *see* Fielding, M., "Against Competition", *Proceedings of the Philosophy of Education Society of Great Britain*, Vol. X (1976); and on art, Gallie, W.B., "Art as an Essentially Contested Concept", *Philosophical Quarterly*, Vol. 6 (1956).
3. For attempts to classify and explicate the notion of a game, *see*, for example, Groos, K., *The Play of Man* (Heinemann, 1901); Huizinga, J., *Homo Ludens* (Beacon Press, 1955); and Caillois, R., *Man, Play and Games* (Thames & Hudson, 1962).

4. Huizinga, J., *op. cit.*, p.203.

5. Caillois, R., *Man, Play and Games.*

6. Cf. Bailey, C., "Games, Winning and Education", *Cambridge Journal of Education,* Vol. 5 (1975), p.47.

7. *See* Aspin, D.N., "Ethical Aspects of Sport and Games", *Proceedings of the Philosophy of Education Society of Great Britain,* Vol. IX (1975).

8. This is not to be taken to imply that we regard dance as *logically* a part of physical education. On the contrary, we are firmly of the opinion that it belongs properly within the field of the arts; but we recognise that, in practice (owing largely to historical accident), dance in schools is often treated as a physical education activity.

9. *op. cit.*, p.44.

10. *ibid.*, p.48.

11. Aspin, D.N., "Games, Winning and Education: Some Further Comments", *Cambridge Journal of Education,* Vol. 5 (1975), p.52.

12. *See* Veal, A.J., "Sport and Recreation in England and Wales. An analysis of adult participation patterns", in *Sports Council Research Memorandum,* No. 74, 1977.

13. *See* footnote 12.

14. Cf. Dearden, R., *The Philosophy of Primary Education* (Routledge & Kegan Paul, 1968), p.99.

CHAPTER 2

The Complexity of Games

Young children's interests and endeavours in the realm of physical activity are easy to recognise since they are immediately and readily observable. There is no need to devise tests, draw up questionnaires or conduct interviews to discover their basic need for bodily action and their love of many kinds of movement. Everywhere, in the street, in the playground and even in the classroom, there is abundant evidence of their enjoyment of the sensation of motion and of their satisfaction in and desire for physical skill.

We may, for example, see them vigorously whirling round and round and then flopping to the ground, rhythmically beating their arms against their sides, gently rocking, swaying or bouncing up and down. Wherever there is water children may be seen not only splashing and dabbling, pouring and measuring it, and so on, but also pushing through it, testing its resistance and buoyancy in relation to their own bodies and generally exploring movement possibilities which belong to that particular medium. Walls, trees, fences, chairs, stairs and the like stimulate such things as climbing, balancing, scrambling, swinging, hanging, sliding and jumping on, over and off. Running, jumping and throwing are three activities in which many children like to engage in such a way as to try to improve on previous performances, and they find pleasure too in becoming dextrous with objects which can be set in motion — kicking cans or stones, for instance, aiming and juggling with pebbles and striking at them in the air with a stick, bowling tyres along and so forth. Sometimes these last pursuits lead to competitive play involving the making of rules and the scoring of points, either against one opponent or more, although often the concern is simply with acquiring skill in relation to moving objects and with attempting to beat their own record rather than striving to beat others.

Such activities may be related to the major branches of physical education, namely dance,[15] swimming, gymnastics, athletics and games respectively. Dance typically involves engaging in rhythmical and patterned movement for its own sake; swimming, gymnastics and athletics, using the body in a skilful way in relation to the physical environment; games dealing with an object in motion, sometimes with an implement, in order to defeat an opponent or opponents within a framework of rules. It is important to recognise the complexity of this last type of activity, especially where, in contrast to a game such as marbles, the players themselves are on the move in large spaces.

First, the actual *physical* demands are considerable, since constant adaptation is necessary to a flying, rolling or bouncing ball, quoit or shuttle, together with skill in manoeuvring it in some way. General bodily agility has therefore to be combined with manipulative dexterity in relation to *an object in motion* (which is not a requirement of dance, swimming, gymnastics or athletics). Moreover, in a game not only is the player on the move himself, but often he also has to adapt to others, whether members of his own side or opponents, who themselves are on the move. Spaces frequently alter in shape and size, and timing is all-important; a burst of speed, a momentary hesitation or an abrupt halt may be called for; sudden swerves, about-turns and rapid changes of direction are often required; lunging and reaching occur in all games, and sometimes leaping, crouching and diving as well; in some instances feet as well as hands must be able to control the ball; and whenever an implement is used the co-ordination necessary is even more complex.

Next, a game (as defined in the Preface) involves at least one opponent against whom one endeavours to pit one's wits as well as one's skill in order to win. If there is more than one a side, then, in addition, co-operation with another or several is needed: one becomes part of a larger whole striving to beat a pair or group composed similarly of individual units. Tactical play correspondingly develops in complexity, and the judging of situations and making of decisions take on new proportions. Thus a certain level of *cognitive* and *social* development is essential.

Finally, but by no means of least importance, is the fact that competition implies the understanding and voluntary acceptance of a code of rules governing methods of play and scoring and, if there is an independent umpire or referee, a readiness to abide by his verdicts. In other words a degree of *moral* awareness is required: one freely undertakes to keep certain promises and to fulfil certain obligations.

If, however, we now consider all this against the background of what is in general believed to characterise the various stages of children's development in our society, it becomes apparent that at the Infant and lower Junior stages there are difficulties in respect of all these features of games.

Physical features

In the first place, although a considerable degree of bodily mastery has already been achieved before a child arrives at school at all, skill in adapting to *changing* situations is obviously limited. He is able, that is, to walk, run, jump, balance on things, and climb and scramble up and down, on and off, through, along and over them so long as they are relatively stable (adjustment to a mobile piece of apparatus is far less easy). But sudden stopping, sharp changes of direction and jumping while looking upward are generally beyond him, even when timing in relation to a moving object or another person is not involved.

Similarly, while most children before reaching school age already possess a certain amount of skill in handling a variety of tools and materials, binocular vision and co-ordination of hand and eye are far from fully developed and there is generally less control of small muscles than of large ones. Consequently, coping with things in motion such as balls, hoops or quoits, which bounce, spin, roll or may be airborne for shorter or longer periods, presents problems of a kind which are not encountered in dealing with, for example, paint-brushes, scissors or percussion instruments. Because these are not themselves moving they do not demand major adjustments of the whole body, nor the making of quick decisions to meet, avoid or retrieve them. To hit or propel a ball with a bat or stick of some sort, or to strike a shuttle, is even more taxing, since contact is intermittent and the implement itself has also to be managed.

During the Infant school stage manipulative skill increases considerably and, as the child becomes more generally agile, getting to the right place at the right time becomes less of a chancy business. Nevertheless, to adapt to several other moving players and the situations which are thus produced, while at the same time keeping an object under control, is no easy achievement for lower, or even upper Juniors — yet these are precisely the main features of games such as netball and football or the simplified versions of these that may be played.

Cognitive and social features

It is obvious, too, that to attempt to outplay another (or others), and to function competently as a member of a team, particularly one consisting of several players, requires a level of cognitive and social maturity which is well beyond what can usually be expected at the Primary school stage. To grasp something of the pattern of a game as a whole and to envisage likely developments of a particular manoeuvre; to see things from another's point of view and to recognise courses of action open to other players; and in appreciating the demands of a situation to be prepared to submerge one's personal desires in the interests of the team as a whole — these are hardly well-developed attributes of children under eleven.

This is not to suggest that children of approximately seven, and older, have little capacity for co-operation in general. On the contrary, their readiness and ability to assist one another in the acquisition of skill, as well as to engage in projects of an imaginative nature and those which afford opportunities for joint investigation and discovery, are striking, and perhaps still tend to be underestimated and insufficiently catered for in some schools. But co-operation in terms of the teamwork necessary for many games is largely outside their scope, and in a legislated situation involving the somewhat arbitrary assignment of roles, the need for which may not be clear, it is not surprising that success is often limited. Collaboration between players is apt to be of a rather primitive kind and a so-called team of, say, three will function, in fact, as *three ones* rather than *one three* for a considerable time.

Moral features

Lastly, engaging with others in play of the kind that is based on mutually agreed terms is in general beyond the scope of most children in their early school years, since at this stage the ability to understand the nature and function of rules, let alone consistently abide by them, is not well developed. It is indeed well known that Infants usually play *alongside* rather than *against* one another, at first neither co-operating nor competing on any common basis. They may engage in an activity similar to that of their neighbours, but in the early stages it remains a largely private affair which may be modified from time to time without reference to anyone else.

This is still the case when they begin to share in combined enterprises. Doing what others do — or seem to do — becomes of greater importance; but in attempting to take part in the play of older children or those more experienced than themselves, young ones are able less to participate in a game conducted according to common consent than to imitate its external features while continuing to follow their own "rules". Relative scores are of little interest, and winning or losing of no consequence — if, indeed, they are recognised at all as the point of the activity.

Most young children, of course, are no less keen to achieve excellence in this field of endeavour than in any other. If, for instance, they are asked how many times they can bounce a ball, they often claim fantastic accomplishments; but even when they can count accurately and take as much pleasure in using their newly-gained mastery in games-like activities as in any other appropriate situation, keeping a score in relation to others is usually of slight importance compared with the activity itself and their personal skill.

However, the ability — though not necessarily the desire — to compete on mutually agreed terms becomes increasingly evident throughout the Junior school, and when an activity begins to be regarded as something that involves following the same procedure as everyone else in order to win, within a framework that must first be settled, a new stage of considerable significance has started — one, indeed, that brings to the fore the whole issue of obliging children to engage in an activity competitively. Nevertheless, during this period when "fixing things up"[16] for the purposes of play, whether competitive or non-competitive, may become of interest (i.e. establishing the ways in which an activity is to be regulated), each individual is still apt to continue to play his own version in spite of an apparent measure of agreement having been reached. Though the intention to observe the rules is genuine enough, the ability to do so may be lacking, and there is often little recognition among children of their failure in this respect.

Piaget found with boys playing marbles that, even up to ten or eleven, children of the same age and even the same class were apt, when questioned, to proffer varying and often conflicting accounts of what should, or should not, happen — each had a purely personal conception of the rules although there was an obvious desire for mutual understanding and fair play. It is only at the next stage, when rules become of importance in themselves and interest is taken in settling disputes and legislating for all circumstances, that children may be said to have grasped fully the notion of a game (as earlier defined).

Little, if any, systematic research appears to have been carried out in relation to children's understanding of games, whether these are formally regulated and taught by adults or invented by children themselves. Yet obviously such considerations are of fundamental importance in any debate on the place and teaching of games within a comprehensive physical education programme in Primary and Middle schools. A good deal more needs to be known about the ways in which children develop an awareness of the need for rules and the ability to formulate and respect them, as well as about their changing attitudes towards their origins and mutability. It would be valuable, for instance, to know how the development of British children's understanding of the rules applying to games of the sort here under discussion compares with that of the boys and girls from Geneva who were the subject of Piaget's investigations in the nineteen-thirties in respect of marbles.

The experience of the authors suggests that, in the case of children in this country (perhaps because of belonging to a society and an era heavily influenced by sport), the various stages succeed one another rather more quickly. This means that some children of nine and the majority of ten-year olds appreciate that games rules are matters of agreement and thus capable of alteration. If offered the opportunity, children of this age and upwards often show not only interest but also ability in inventing their own rules and playing accordingly.

The various demands of a game, then — physical, cognitive, social and moral — begin to come within the capacity of children only at approximately the upper Junior stage; any real "maturity" in this sphere before then is unusual. In view of this we shall therefore now consider the type of provision and organisation of games activity that seems appropriate at Infant and Junior levels — proposals that are also relevant, we believe, to the teaching of children in Middle schools as well as those at the lower Secondary stage.

Notes

15. *See* footnote 8.
16. Piaget, J., *The Moral Judgment of the Child* (Routledge & Kegan Paul, 1932).

CHAPTER 3

Implications for Learning

That the teaching of games in the Primary school tends to be completely out of line with what is characteristic of teaching in other areas of the curriculum is easily illustrated; indeed it is hardly necessary to look beyond other branches of physical education (as is often conceded by teachers themselves).

In dance, for example, children of this age range are not typically required to conform to a particular style or to learn ready-made dances originated by adults; in swimming the mastery of specific strokes is not usually the immediate concern; in gymnastics it is not demanded that every individual should achieve a limited number of prescribed feats of agility in a stylised way; and in athletics concentrating on the highly specific techniques peculiar to the various events is not expected. Similarly, with language, mathematics, science, art and craft, and so on, the teacher does not rely exclusively on methods of direct instruction, important though these are at any level, but usually seeks also to foster young children's interest in and curiosity about themselves and their environment through the provision of a variety of materials and situations: they are helped to learn to a considerable extent by means of exploration, experiment and discovery.

At a later stage, when demonstration and instruction are likely to assume an increasingly prominent role, children are nevertheless still encouraged to find out for themselves, to ask questions, to solve problems, to investigate at first hand how certain things are related, and to use their powers of inventiveness and imagination both alone and with others. In most physical education activities, therefore, the teacher does not invariably lay down exactly what is to be done and how, but often presents a framework whereby pupils select from a range of possibilities, meet a series of challenges, and acquire a "vocabulary" on which to draw in order to create their own dances and sequences of movement in the water or with apparatus.

There is, of course, a place in the Primary school, especially with older children, for the teaching of specific techniques. Thus within physical education children will probably be required eventually to learn, say, certain swimming strokes, step combinations, balances and turning jumps, although sometimes their own inventions and solutions to problems may result in the performance of sequences not unlike those of a recognisably conventional kind.

But the interests of the majority at this stage remain wide rather than narrowly specialist, and their curiosity, whether about water finding its own level, the habits of hamsters, or the differing behaviour of a hard, bouncy ball and an airflow one, is in general boundless. They are eager to try almost anything, and Juniors especially, unlike many older children, are usually prepared to tackle a vast range of physical activities; unless required to strive for standards well beyond their capacity to achieve the majority rarely seem inclined to accept, or even to recognise, their limitations.

It therefore seems desirable that in the sphere of games too they should be given opportunities to participate in a variety of pursuits rather than confined to a few adult inventions; that through experimenting with apparatus of a diverse and less conventional kind as well as with the traditional sort, and discovering effective ways of using it, they become skilful on a wide front rather than drilled in a restricted number of highly-specialised techniques; that they are guided towards a recognition of certain features common to all games (*see* Chapter 4); and that instead of being required always to conform to ready-made games involving rules for which they frequently see no reason and which they may not understand, they are sometimes challenged to use their ingenuity to devise games activities of their own in which the need for rules arises directly.

To share ultimately in the process of making a new game

or a variation of one already known, finding answers to problems arising and then playing it according to mutual consent, would seem to be at least as educationally valuable as learning only traditional games with already formulated rules. There is more likelihood, too, that as conformity to adult ideas and standards is not demanded, a spirit of fun may prevail rather than either an over-serious or an indifferent attitude.

Moreover, the games situation, like any other sphere of learning, can afford an opportunity for the teacher to increase his knowledge of children as individuals. For when the range of activities is increased and personal invention is encouraged, new insights into children's abilities and preferences may be gained. This is not so likely if all are engaged in the same stereotyped pursuits. Indeed, the teacher's view of any one child may be adversely affected because of that child's failure to deal with the requirements of a conventional game. Some children, then, may be observed to excel at games of an *airborne* nature, others at those which are mainly *along the ground*; some may be at their best *with an implement*, others *without*; some will probably favour *running* games, others the *batting* or *net* type (*see* Chapter 4 for definitions of these terms). Not only may such things contribute to the teacher's total picture of an individual, but the child too may find satisfaction and confidence in the fact that in this sphere as well as in others he has different kinds of opportunity to prove himself. (More will be said on this later.)

It will be clear from what has been said in the previous chapter about the complexities of a game (as originally defined) that among both Infant and Junior children there is likely to be in any one age group a wide range of ability and interest in the various aspects of this area of physical education. In order, however, to assist the teacher to plan broadly for successive periods of development, reference will be made to four stages at the Primary level which it is suggested are fairly easy to recognise.

1. Young infants

When children enter the Infant school some will, of course,

already be familiar with at least some types of games equipment, especially balls, and, usually as a result of the influence of older members of the family, may have become relatively "conditioned" to using it in a conventional manner. It is common, however, when provided with a wider selection of apparatus than that usually found in the home, and left to play freely with an assortment of bats, quoits, shuttlecocks and targets of various kinds, as well as balls, for young children not to discriminate between the different kinds of play which each affords.

Thus just as, for instance, a climbing frame may be treated as a castle or a jungle and not as a piece of agility equipment for use as conceived of by the gymnast, or cymbals initially provided for musical or dance experience be transformed into headgear, so games apparatus is frequently used in what, to the specialist, is not essentially a games-like way. Balls may be thrown behind the back, under the legs, placed between the feet for jumping or rolled back and forth with the toes (sometimes, it would seem, for the sheer pleasure of the sensation); hoops may be used not for aiming, but for bowling, spinning round the waist, or getting through and jumping in and around; quoits may be twirled around the arms, placed on the head like a halo, or squeezed and twisted (again, perhaps largely for their sensory appeal).

Activities of a gymnastic nature may thus overlap with those related more directly to certain aspects of games, and both types with play of the fantasy or sensory kind. As the Plowden Report of 1967 pointed out (para. 706), ". . . it will not always be easy to separate different modes of movement experience." Neither does it seem desirable in the very early stages to attempt to do so, since general experience of handling small apparatus is likely to precede its more specialised use.

However, the recommendations of the Plowden Committee that movement teaching will (does this imply *should*?) be "more closely related to specific ends" only by the time children leave the Primary school is, in our opinion, questionable. It would seem rather that by the beginning of the Junior stage, at least, dance, gymnastics and games require the provision of separate periods (though this may not be possible weekly), each with a certain unity of objectives. Much of course depends upon the facilities of the school and the availability of equipment, as well as on the allocation of time for physical education as a whole; but a more clear-cut distinction between the various branches, and the aims of each, might do much to prevent the confusion at present evident among teachers as to their function within each type of lesson and the kind of experience and understanding they are setting out to give.

With young Infants, however, the chief need is for plenty of opportunities to use a wide range of apparatus, and just as in art education, for instance, a variety of materials of contrasting colours, textures and shapes is provided, there should be games equipment of many kinds and of differing weight, construction and size.[17] Nevertheless, the limitations of such apparatus for young children have to be recognised; all-round bodily exercise, as indicated earlier, can be catered for far more satisfactorily through dance, swimming and activities stimulated by agility apparatus of the climbing, scrambling and swinging type. Moreover, while perception of depth and hand-eye co-ordination are immature, and manipulative dexterity comparatively undeveloped, play with moving objects is apt to be restricting and even frustrating; indeed with young children it often amounts to little more than the retrieving of wayward balls.

As mentioned in the previous chapter, much of the early exploratory play of children is of an individual kind, and though it is often carried on alongside others, these companions seem to serve more as an audience for whatever is being pursued, together with the accompanying commentaries, than as anything else; it is also apt, to some extent, to lack continuity and purposefulness. Children of course differ a good deal in this respect, some persisting with the same piece of equipment over comparatively long periods of time and perhaps repeating the same activity over and over again, others continually varying what they do with it or flitting rapidly from one activity to the next. This not merely affords the teacher further information about the individuals with whom he has to deal, but calls for judgment on his part as to the amount and kind of freedom of choice to allow the class as a whole or certain members of it. It is not unknown for some children in a reception class, for instance, to be so overwhelmed by a superabundance of apparatus and unlimited choice as to be almost paralysed into inactivity, while others, by contrast, may become over-stimulated and find it difficult to settle for even a few minutes at one particular occupation.

The teacher's first job, therefore, as far as games experience is concerned, is to ensure a plentiful but judicious supply of objects and implements of suitable dimensions which can be struck, thrown, caught or propelled along — tenniquoits, shuttlecocks, balls of varying sizes and weights, and oval as well as round; bats and sticks of differing lengths and shapes; and targets such as skittles, stumps, hoops, rings and wall- and ground-markings. This does not imply that every type of equipment which the school possesses must be available every lesson, though in most cases a good assortment is desirable. Part of the teacher's responsibility is to decide whether there is to be complete freedom of choice, both of apparatus and of the use to which it is put, or whether any limitations are to be placed on either. He may also be obliged to structure the situation so that both large agility apparatus and small games-like equipment are provided simultaneously, in which case he must also consider the balance between each, and again whether the kind of activity is to be selected by the individual.

As in other realms of experience, the teacher should constantly be prepared to stimulate fresh exploration and investigation and so lead children, as appropriate, to further stages of mastery and understanding. In the previous chapter it was pointed out that controlling moving objects directly with the body is a good deal easier than striking and manoeuvring them with an implement. With young children, therefore, he should encourage the use of heads and feet in addition to fists, palms and fingers, before concentrating on attempts to foster interest and ability in using various sorts of bats, rackets and sticks.

2. Upper Infants and Lower Juniors

Throughout the Infant and lower Junior school, what is of most importance from the children's point of view is the fun and challenge of discovering the manifold possibilities of the apparatus itself, acquiring skill in managing it in a variety of ways, and becoming familiar with its behaviour in relation to the manner in which it is used. Towards the end of the Infant stage most children may be expected not merely to play in an exploratory fashion with equipment with which they are well acquainted, but to seek to increase their mastery of particular techniques through constant repetition of the same activity, such as aiming at a mark on a wall or pat-bouncing a ball with a bat as many times as possible.

This is where *practice*, as such, has its place. This is a vital means by which children learn and also satisfy their desire for skill as an end in itself; but although practice is often self-motivated, encouragement and help in achieving the desired end are also sometimes necessary. At this stage too some children are able to devise their own games — games, however, that are not so much contests involving rules and outplaying others, but more in the nature of tests of their own ability in which they compete, as it were, against themselves, with a particular objective (such as keeping a ball in the air in a special way, using an implement or a part of the body), and a simple system of scoring.

Alongside this concern with personal achievement, however, there is usually an increasing interest in what others, especially older children, do, and upper Infants are often eager to join in the games of more experienced playmates. It is thus that they are likely to become acquainted with games rules, which to begin with are for them little more than an outline of what is "the done thing". But although on the whole anxious to conform, they are unable to appreciate the binding nature of a rule and the idea of striving to win by observing certain conditions.

Even though they tend to remain "on the fringe", playing on their own terms, it seems desirable from the teacher's point of view to foster this kind of situation when it occurs spontaneously (as is likely with vertical grouping) provided it can be of benefit all round. Many older children are remarkably good-natured and tolerant on such occasions, and seem to enjoy encouraging the younger ones in these delusions and making it possible for them to appear to gain success.

In the main, then, co-operation in the early stages is not of the kind described in the previous chapter in connection with the requirements of that kind of game which entails collabora-ation with another (or others) with the common aim of out-witting an opponent (or opponents), but implies a loose association of individuals interested chiefly in increasing their own range of skill. A partner who will send a ball or quoit opens up all sorts of new possibilities and thus provides exciting new challenges. It is his usefulness for such purposes which counts, rather than his potential as a player with whom a game can be conducted on mutually agreed terms; and he for his part will, for instance, obligingly pitch an object in such a way as to make it easy or progressively more difficult for his partner to strike or collect it successfully. Many children of six and seven often engage spontaneously in activities of this kind involving two, three or four together, and in the past their ability to do so has perhaps been under-rated by many teachers.

These pursuits are not games as originally defined, though they do contain elements akin to them. For their social and moral features are usually markedly different; and it is this difference which it is essential for the adult, with his pre-conceived notions of competition and rules as indispensable ingredients of school games activities, to recognise in his dealings with young children. If they say, "Let's have a game of football," they rarely mean that they are about to embark on a duel between opposing sides, with the intention of achieving a result and establishing a winner. They are more likely to mean (and may often be heard to say), "Let's play kicking" (or heading, hitting, catching, etc.) or, at a later stage, "Let's have a game of passing" (or dodging, guarding the goal, and so on).

In other words, it is the activity itself which is of major importance, and we should note here that the appeal for many is twofold: there is a delight not only in acquiring skill, but also in the physical actions of running, leaping, hurling oneself at an object, diving to the ground and so forth. All this tends to be done in a vigorous, full-blooded manner (especially perhaps in the case of boys), and on a scale often beyond the requirements of the situation itself, as for instance when a lunge to catch a ball or make a save as a "goalkeeper" leads to rolling over and over or to balancing in a spectacular fashion.

Though such enterprises may include keeping a personal score, having begun to count children frequently forget to continue to do so. The lack of significance which a true score has for them is well illustrated by the case of three children of about eight years of age who, absorbed in a "game" of the cricket type, were found to be adding together not only their runs, but the number of times a wicket fell, and so reached a cumulative score of 80 for 11 with no little satisfaction!

At the upper Infant and lower Junior levels, therefore, the teacher has a vital role to play in structuring situations in which individuals and/or small groups continue to explore new ways of using apparatus, especially new combinations of various pieces, and are given the chance to extend and consolidate skilfulness through simple repetition (with and without scoring) and games-like activities in association with others. The classification of games suggested in Chapter 4, together with an analysis of the fundamental types of activity involved, is designed to assist him in this task, as well as to indicate a means by which developing skill may be assessed.

A good deal of knowledge about the relationship between a particular action and the resulting behaviour of a ball, quoit or shuttle may be gained incidentally during such play, although for some time a child may be unable to express such knowledge in words. An indication of progress in this respect is the extent to which he becomes interested in reflecting on cause and effect; in trying deliberately to achieve a specific result, such as varying the trajectory of a quoit; and in finding out, for example, where to aim a ball in order to bounce it continuously on the run without losing speed.

3. Middle Junior

It is, however, chiefly in the middle and upper Junior school that opportunities should be presented for systematic experimentation and problem-solving in connection with the games-like activities referred to above, and for the sort of experience which draws attention to the factors common to games. A fuller treatment of these considerations is given in Chapters 8 and 9.

A further development which may begin to manifest itself during this stage involves the idea of trying to beat others by doing the same as they do and abiding by fixed laws. Whereas at first children are able only to delineate the broad features of a game in terms of what is to be done (for example, "You throw the ball for me to hit and I run to that post before you get it"), they now begin to incorporate elementary notions of obligation and fair play of a less rough and ready kind than previously. "You have to (do so and so) . . . and you can (do such and such . . . but not . . .) and if you (do this or that) you have to . . . ." Such rules, which may be quite complicated, tend, however, to be frequently changed not only from one occasion to the next but as play actually proceeds. This is partly because they are usually evolved during the course of the activity itself as the needs of the situation demand, rather than established beforehand through discussion, and partly because, as we have already seen, each individual is apt to persist with his own idea of the game, which is thus often at variance with that of others.

Indeed at this stage the whole business of rule-making and rule-keeping is only imperfectly understood, and whatever games procedures children might seem to grasp tend to be followed inconsistently. For rules are not yet conceived of as part of a contract freely entered into and negotiated and hence capable of being modified. They may even, as Piaget has suggested, have something of a sacred character, appearing to be invested with an almost divine authority: when questioned, children seem to regard them as absolute laws issuing from some external source and never to be altered. But in practice they are not always aware of when they are abiding by them and when they are not. It is thus no matter for surprise that when young children are presented with ready-made rules in games, especially in isolation and not as the occasion requires, many regularly "break" them.

What seems appropriate at this level, therefore, is that priority should be given to the *co-operative* aspects of games play on the basis of the various types of activity and means of experimenting with apparatus discussed in the following chapters. In this way time may continue to be devoted to playing *with* rather than *against* others, and concentration focused upon the acquisition of skill in larger groups than previously; opportunities for the exercise of ingenuity in respect of rule-making belong more properly to a later period and will be referred to in Chapter 8. At the stage of development of which we are now speaking, although the teacher may from time to time encourage the children themselves to settle problems of procedure, or to do so with his assistance, their limited understanding of rules justifies his sometimes stepping in promptly with arbitrary solutions in order that play may be interrupted as little as possible.

4. Upper Juniors

When children reach the upper Junior stage they usually begin to show a greater concern for the "right way" of doing things, and games techniques are no exception. They want to know about correct grips, how to place the feet in certain circumstances, how to collect and throw a rugby ball most efficiently, and so forth. Both boys and girls are often keen to emulate high-class players and to model their style on theirs; they are also very prepared to bring their powers of observation to bear on differences between one method and another, to detect faults in performance and to discover basic principles governing success in controlling objects and implements.

At the same time the major games are likely to command their attention to some extent, especially in localities where sporting interests are strong and perhaps a particular team occasions fervent partisan loyalty. Group activities tend to take on a new significance, and winning and losing begin to assume more importance, though throughout the Primary school, unless prematurely fomented by adults, this usually seems to be secondary to the concern for being in action, having plenty of turns and so forth.

Nevertheless it is at this stage that the question of compulsory games becomes acute. For once the individual is aware that the point of a game is to win, that its rules are alterable and, together with its methods of play and scoring, designed specifically for the purpose of outpointing, i.e. defeating, an opponent or opponents, he cannot justifiably be blamed if he dislikes such enterprises and, given the choice, declines to take part. To repeat what has already been pointed out in Chapter 1, since of its very nature a game involves *freely* undertaking certain obligations and abiding by certain constraints, to suppose that anyone can genuinely *play* a game under duress is logically absurd; he merely "goes through the motions".

If, however, the guide-lines set out in this book are adopted, no one need engage in competitive play, yet at the same time sufficient experience will have been gained for children to come to see what is involved in games as a whole, as well as in particular types of games, and thus be able to make a choice that is not uninformed either in terms of whether to continue to take part or, if they do, in which sorts of activity. *What follows in this section thus applies only to those children who have freely exercised such a choice.* And for them it would seem desirable to continue to cast the net widely as regards the types of game that are possible and to ensure necessary modifications of the adult variety.

With upper Juniors greater emphasis can be placed on the cognitive features of games play, but it is nevertheless still important for the teacher to appreciate that the general desire for energetic activity continues unabated (indeed it is perhaps difficult to overlook this fact!). So also does the desire for skill, though this now becomes more a means of "having a good game" than an end in itself, and with some children begins to include tactical considerations. Simply to throw or hit a ball as hard as possible, or to try to run faster than everyone else, no longer always satisfies. Manoeuvres designed to lead an opponent to expect something which does not in fact happen, such as drawing him into a position and then placing the object out of his reach, begin to be appreciated, especially in those situations in which such deception can be practised by a single individual as distinct from those that depend on having an understanding with others.

Interest also develops in what constitutes fair play, what

should be allowed and what should not, how offenders should be penalised, what system of scoring is best to adopt, and other similar considerations. Details of this sort are now recognised as matters which must be settled and understood by all, but which can be changed and adapted provided that this is done with the consent of the majority and will improve the game. As well as dealing with such contingencies pragmatic- ally, many upper Juniors (like Middle and lower Secondary school children) enjoy *discussing* these topics; this of course does not have to be confined to the playground or games field, nor occupy time set aside specifically for games. With appropriate stimulation and guidance they can thus become enthusiastic about making variations on familiar games and keen to invent new ones (*see* Appendix).

To some extent this is a continuation of what has already gone on at earlier stages, but whereas then rules were manipul- ated rather unreflectively in order to get on with the process of playing, they now become of interest in their own right. Piaget speaks of children at this stage (approximately eleven to twelve in the case of his Geneva subjects) taking "a peculiar pleasure in anticipating all possible cases and codifying them" and in "complicating things at will". Though at first it will probably be found that Juniors seem to favour any form of legislation which makes for more turns, more activity, more share in the game, they eventually show signs of being pre- pared to consider not only procedure but principle — not merely what works and is expedient, but what is "right".

Suggestions about ways in which the teacher might regul- ate proceedings so as to help children to invent their own games are given in some detail in Chapter 8, along with points to be considered in guiding experiments and posing problems, as already mentioned. Meanwhile the following summary sets out the main characteristics of the four stages outlined in this chapter and indicates the kind of opportunities and ex- perience which it accordingly seems desirable to provide.

Stage I (Young Infants). Exploratory play of a somewhat undifferentiated kind with a variety of apparatus, chiefly individually but in the company of others.

Stage II (Upper Infants and lower Juniors). Interest in acquisition of skill as an end in itself both individually and with others, beating own score, etc. Some interest in older children's games and playing "on the fringe" of these.

Stage III (Middle Juniors). Desire for personal skill persists, but more in relation to playing a "game" with others; elementary rule-making and beginnings of interest in why apparatus behaves as it does.

Stage IV (Upper Juniors). Among those who show an interest in playing "proper" games in which competing with others on equal terms is important, desire for skill intensifies in relation to the type of game in question; interest in experimenting with apparatus in particular ways and problem-solving continues; concern with precise rules develops and tactics begin to engage the attention of some.

It must, of course, be strongly emphasised that such suggestions are of necessity only a rather rough and ready guide, and that any attempt to correlate these stages of interest and development with chronological age is bound to be somewhat tentative. Children differ in their abilities and rates of progress in games at least as much as in any other sphere, and further detailed investigation on a larger scale than has been possible here is obviously necessary. Much might be done by teachers, in the absence of formal research, to confirm or modify these findings, and, indeed, if games experience is to be taken at all seriously as a part of Primary education it is obvious that observation and recording of levels of achievement and progress are as essential as in, for example, reading or mathematics.

In the past little interest in such assessment seems to have been shown by teachers — yet another indication of the ambivalent position occupied by games (and, indeed, other physical education activities) in education. As we have seen, on the one hand they are widely, and sometimes unquestioningly, accepted as part of the curriculum; on the other, when it comes to the reporting of pupils' ability and progress few details are supplied, and then only in terms of the sketchiest of criteria. But since today every teacher's accountability in relation to what he teaches is rightly being stressed, the importance of keeping records in all subjects is at last being recognised as essential. Some suggestions as to what might constitute progressive understanding and achievement in respect of games may be found in this book, and no doubt the discerning teacher will both select from these and supplement them with information from other sources as well as from his own experience and investigations.

Whether a child needs the chance simply to play freely; finds it sufficiently satisfying to play alone, keeping a score or not as the case may be; seeks to join in with others, either "on the fringe" or more fully; likes to compete against an opponent, to collaborate with another to beat others and to take an active part in a game for several players; is able to understand what constitutes fair play and to abide by rules, and so on, reflects something of his overall personality as well as his progress in this particular area, and might well be compared with evidence collected from other situations.

In order to make competent assessments and to plan a comprehensive games programme, particularly for children reaching the stage of wanting to master particular skills and being able to recognise fundamental similarities and differences between various types of games and the activities of which they consist, it is necessary for the teacher to take a fresh look at these. The next chapter aims at helping him to do so.

Notes

17. Details of items suitable for use in Primary schools are given in Chapter 7.

CHAPTER 4

A Classification of Games

In all games of the kind we are examining, an object of some sort is manoeuvred with either an implement or part of the body, and aimed in relation to a goal or target, or a space or other players. This always involves one or more of the following activities:

(a) *sending away* the object, that is, striking or throwing it in some way;
(b) *gaining possession* of the object, that is, catching or collecting it;
(c) *travelling with* the object, that is, carrying or propelling it along.

This chapter deals in turn with each of these from a general point of view, and Chapter 6 with more technical considerations arising from them which should be of direct practical assistance in teaching. Reference is made to some of the well-known games so that the reader may more easily recognise the relationship between theory and practice, and also because it will be found that the games which children devise often resemble those of adults in terms of the *activities* involved.

In order to assist thinking along these lines the classification given below has been evolved. It is hoped that this will enable the teacher to appreciate the factors common to a number of games rather than view each game as an isolated unit.

Category 1.
(In the text these are referred to as "net" games.)
Games in which all players are concerned mainly with *striking*. Here the territory is divided and sides are equal. Examples: badminton, tennis and volleyball.[18]

Category 2.
(In the text these are referred to as "batting" games.)
Games in which the concern of the *batting side* is wholly with *striking* while that of the *fielders* is with *throwing, catching* and *collecting*. This occurs in games such as baseball, cricket, rounders and stoolball, in which territory is shared inasmuch as the running track of the batsmen is part of the total area in which both teams play. In these games either one or more of the batting side compete against the complete fielding team.

Category 3.
(In the text these are referred to as "running" games.)
Games in which *both* teams are engaged in *throwing* or *striking* AND *catching* or *collecting* AND *carrying* or *propelling along*. Here two numerically equal sides compete and territory is shared. Examples: basketball, football, hockey, lacrosse, netball[19] and rugby.

1. Striking and throwing

The term *striking* is intended to cover heading and kicking as well as all kinds of hitting, whether with hand or implement, and *throwing* to include bowling, although in practice the two have to be distinguished. They are dealt with first since they are basic to all games-like activities and indeed are the sole concern of some.

Important differences exist between hitting an oncoming object and striking a ball already under the control, or at least partial control, of the player. In throwing, the ball is, of course, already in the player's possession. These differences will later be seen to have significance in the planning of children's games experience. In many respects, however, there are basic similarities between these activities. It may not immediately be obvious that they are essentially all forms of aiming, since this is often assumed to be related to a fixed goal or target. Yet on reflection it will be appreciated that *where* the object goes is always of importance, and within the context of games as a whole the purposes and kinds of aiming are more diverse than might first be imagined. Not only are striking and throwing in themselves *the means of scoring,* but they contribute largely to *the manoeuvring of the ball* into a position favourable for a shot at goal in those games in which scoring must occur within specified areas; they are also sometimes *the means of preventing scoring.*

Although the initial intention of a player attempting to strike a ball is to make contact with it, he sooner or later becomes interested in directing it so that it falls beyond a certain point, or reaches another player, or a space or, of course, the goal itself or even a particular part of it. Any throw, hit or kick eventually has a destination of some kind, whether this is precisely defined or not, and all passing therefore involves aiming. The "target" in the case of another member of the team may be stationary or on the move, and in all games spaces change in size and shape to a greater or lesser extent as play proceeds.

In games belonging to *Category 1,* in which territory is divided and the players separated by a net, attempts are made to place the ball, quoit or shuttle in a space out of reach of the opponent(s). This may be little more than a single spot, in which case a high degree of accuracy is required, or an area at that moment inaccessible to the opposing side within which it may be sufficient to aim somewhat less specifically; there is thus a certain "margin of error" available to the striker, though he needs constantly to try to alter his aim.

Similarly, in games belonging to *Category 2* the batsman strives to send the ball into spaces not covered by the fielders; this may range from quite a large area, which again affords a certain latitude of aim, to a narrow gap between players. For the fielding team also aiming is vital; catching and collecting are rarely sufficient in themselves.[20] The ball must be returned accurately to relatively fixed points, while the bowler of course is required to pitch the ball within well-defined limits, and in cricket and stoolball at a target which he endeavours actually to strike.

In games belonging to *Category 3,* aiming may be recognised as most varied and complex. These all involve passing and eventually a shot at a fixed target, whether this be the comparatively large area of a goal-mouth or the small and high basketball ring. Every player therefore tries to send the ball accurately either into a space or to another player's hands, feet or implement, in order for him to collect it with ease and economy. Since moreover the territory in these games is shared by both sides, which usually consist of a considerable number of players, their positions and therefore the spaces are constantly changing.

The zones into which an object can be directed are numerous, but are often determined by the structure of the game itself and its playing areas. In "net" games the object is aimed towards a comparatively small area which lies in front of the striker as he faces the net.

In "batting" games the rounders or baseball batsman is concerned with sending the ball into an area bounded roughly by a semi-circle and which again is faced as he positions himself to strike. In cricket and stoolball, however, since the wicket lies in the centre of the pitch, the batsman has an area all round him into which he may direct the ball. This striking area is such that the ball may be hit or deflected into a great variety of directions. It may be glanced or turned behind the wicket, angled square on to the batsman, or swept or driven into any part of the field in front of the wicket.

In "running" games, although parallel or backward passes are often made for various tactical reasons, the players in possession pass the ball mainly into a forward direction so that it may progress into the scoring area. (Rugby, of course, is an exception in this respect.)

2. Catching and collecting

The term "gaining possession" has been selected for the purposes of this book in order to emphasise the active nature of the skills involved in all types of receiving a ball or quoit, whether it is then retained momentarily or for a considerable time, and whether hands, feet or an implement are used. It will be apparent that "receiving" in the sense in which it is used for the batsman in cricket or the tennis player awaiting service is therefore not intended in this context, nor are tackling and struggling to maintain possession implied. A distinction needs to be made between catching and collecting, and for convenience "catching" will be defined as gaining control of the ball and holding it while it is in the air, while "collecting" implies that it is travelling along the ground.

In contrast to aiming, which is always concerned with *sending away* an object *from* the player, gaining possession necessarily involves the *gathering* of it *towards* him, sometimes only to a slight extent, at others almost to his body centre. Whereas in the former there is a definite conclusion to the activity, neither catching nor collecting is ever complete in itself in the actual games situation.[21] All kinds of receiving are immediately followed by throwing, hitting or kicking the object, or by carrying or propelling it along.

If we consider again the three categories on page 40 we see that *gaining possession*:

(a) in "net" games *does not occur at all,* except when a quoit is used;
(b) in "batting" games *is the concern of the fielders only,* and is essential to prevent scoring and often to dismiss the batsman;
(c) in "running" games *is the concern of all players,* and is essential both in preventing the opposition from getting the ball and in promoting scoring. In fact catching and collecting, together with throwing and striking, constitute passing. It is in this type of game that not only collecting the ball with the hands occurs but also trapping it with the feet, cradling and fielding it on a stick.

In "batting" games the fielder can rarely know from where to expect the ball until it is struck (or possibly just immediately before, if he can judge from the bowling action or by the way the batsman "shapes up" to meet it), nor indeed whether to expect to be called into action at all. Although it always approaches him from somewhere in front it comes at a variety of speeds, levels and directions both through the air and along and off the ground. He may therefore have to:

(a) *meet the oncoming ball* in a direct line with the point from which it was hit (and, in the case of the wicket-keeper, thrown);

(b) *approach it at an angle*, so cutting off its progress along a line different from that along which he is moving;

(c) *remain stationary* in a position of readiness (as in the case of a close-in fieldsman), waiting to glue his hand to the ball the moment after it leaves the stick or bat.

In all these circumstances he may remain grounded or throw himself into the air or along the ground. A further possibility is that he has to:

(d) *retrieve a ball* which has passed him, pursuing it along the line which it is following.

In "running" games also the player may face an oncoming ball (usually by intercepting a throw, hit or kick from a member of the opposite side), but in addition it may already be travelling in the same general direction as that towards which he is seeking to manoeuvre it, as happens in the case of many passes. This means that as well as collecting, stopping or partially stopping it in order to reverse its progress, he has to be able to receive from both sides, sideways/backwards and even from directly behind him. The ball may also be sent some distance ahead of him, in which case he may run "onto" it without collecting it at all in the true sense, although bringing it under control and steering it on its course without interruption or delay; if, of course, it is trapped or really "caught" on a stick there is inevitably a slight change of direction and loss of time.

In all these cases, however, the player is, generally speaking, more on the attack than on the defence in comparison with the fielder in "batting" games, and is more likely to be able to judge accurately in advance of the ball being passed to him its speed, trajectory and height, as well as the direction from which it is coming.

3. Carrying and propelling

A basic feature of "running" games is that the ball remains for shorter or longer periods in the possession of an individual who "takes it along" with him as he progresses towards his opponents' goal.

This he may do by carrying it in his hands, as in netball and rugby; in an implement, as in lacrosse; by alternately catching and bouncing it, as in basketball; or by propelling it along the ground by a series of taps with feet or stick, as in football and hockey respectively. In the latter instances dribbling, as indeed bouncing, could be regarded as particular forms of striking, but since the player endeavours while on the move to keep the ball to himself, he is not primarily concerned with sending it away towards a target in the same sense as when he kicks, hits or throws it, and the considerations which apply are those rather which obtain in running and carrying.

Differences arise from the fact that while in carrying contact with the ball is *continuous* (a ball cradled in a crosse moves only slightly to and fro), in dribbling and bouncing it is *intermittent*, but in all cases the player is involved in complex sets of skills. He has to maintain an easy and, if possible, fast running action, manipulate the ball and perhaps an implement as well, and dodge, swerve and outmanoeuvre opponents who may tackle him, or at least seek to slow down his progress.

Although, like striking and throwing, these activities of carrying and propelling may in some circumstances be complete in themselves (as when a player scores a point by carrying the ball beyond a certain point, or steers it through the goal while on the run instead of taking a shot at it), they are more often followed by sending away. Since, too, they are always preceded by catching or collecting the ball, changing from one activity to another is closely bound up with the actual skill of running with it.

Finally it may be noted that while "net" and "batting"

games do not demand travelling with the ball,[22] carrying of a kind does occur; in these instances it is the implement (the racket, bat or stick) which must be held as the player moves into new positions or runs between bases or wickets. As this is of some importance it is included in Chapter 6, which deals in further detail with each of the above-listed activities. Next, however, we shall examine the significance of this classification for teaching children of Primary age.

Notes

18. A quoit may also be used in games of this type, but is, of course, thrown not struck.

19. In netball the distance is limited by rules governing the number of steps or leaps a player may take while in possession of the ball, but nevertheless considerable ground may be gained.

20. Exceptions of course occur in cricket and stoolball when, following the dismissal of a batsman, it is not possible also to put out his partner before the next ball is bowled; indeed in cricket the ball becomes virtually "dead" whenever it seems unlikely that a run will be taken. It is interesting to note that in this connection catching and collecting are the wicket-keeper's chief activity, but for the back-stop in rounders throwing is of equal importance.

21. *See* footnote 20.

22. An exception is, of course, in the run-up preceding a bowling action, but carrying the ball is here really incidental to the main activity of bowling and, provided always that the arm and running actions are well co-ordinated, is probably of less importance than the grip with which the ball is held.

CHAPTER 5

Application to Teaching

Having established a scheme for classifying games of the kind in which there is competition between players with an object in motion, and for distinguishing the main types of activity constituting these, we may now survey the implications of such a scheme in relation to children's development as considered earlier.

It would seem that each of the three categories described in Chapter 4 consists both of features which are relatively easy for Primary school children, and of others which present certain difficulties. In some games the advantages of a large playing area may be offset by the smallness of the object, in others the varieties of method by which the object may be manoeuvred by sanctions governing ways of scoring, and so on. Indeed the unique character of any game seems largely to consist in the fascinating balance between those features which afford little difficulty and those which present more of a challenge.

Category 1 games

Since the major "net" games with a ball or shuttle call for striking only, there is little complexity here in terms of the kind of activities involved—that is, catching and collecting, and carrying and propelling, are not demanded. Aiming, moreover, is always within a general area and does not include targets or goals.

Nevertheless, since an oncoming object has to be contended with, a good deal of anticipation and co-ordination is essential, while the use of a racket makes for further complications. If, however, as in volley-ball, instead of having to make an instantaneous decision and return the object immediately to the other side of the net, the player is able to "keep" it in some way, for example, by patting or bouncing it, not only is this difficulty reduced, but a greater range of activity is opened up to the individual. A quoit also provides for variety of action inasmuch as throwing and catching are now required and, as in the case of using balls without an implement, jumping and reaching upward may frequently occur. It is worth noting that games in this category are the only ones which are not restricted to a ball.

From the point of view of the co-operation involved they have much to recommend them for Primary children, since on the one hand they afford opportunities for a certain amount of teamwork of a fairly simple kind when there are several players a side, but on the other allow the individual to act almost entirely independently, while of course in singles each is without commitment to another. Moreover, although upper Juniors can find plenty of interest here in outwitting their opponents by outmanoeuvring them, younger ones can play such games with a minimum of courtcraft; and this is the kind of situation in which their enjoyment of activity, without much regard for the scoring of points, leads them to send the ball or quoit within easy reach of the opposing side so that fairly long rallies can result. The possibility of periods of continuous play, with little time spent in re-starting proceedings after interruption, seems to be an important criterion by which many children judge the merits of a game.

The fact that games belonging to this category cater for small numbers makes for all the players being in action most of the time; it also means that small spaces can be utilised, a rope tied to a post or some kind of fence or railing serving well enough as a "net" at this stage. There is plenty of scope too for modification and invention on the part of the children, and it is noticeable that preconceived ideas about conventional games of this type seem somewhat less common than about those belonging to the other two categories.

There is no reason why, for instance, with large balls, using fists as well as hands should not be allowed, or heading or rolling; juggling and passing with a quoit; or patting and bouncing with a racket, etc. The number of times and for how long such things are to be permitted are matters calling for decision, as also are penalties for infringements and methods of scoring.

Category 2 games

In games of the "batting" kind similar sorts of consideration apply in respect of striking a ball as in the previous category in that it always approaches the player, whether coming directly through the air or bouncing up at him off the ground. But these games always include catching and collecting of all varieties with the hands, and this, like hitting an oncoming ball, poses difficulties for children because of the degree of anticipation and co-ordination required. Unlike those forms of gaining possession in "running" games which are more or less predictable, inasmuch as the ball is often sent deliberately from one player to another, those involved in games of this category are always occasioned by the opposing batsman, and the ball consequently often arrives unexpectedly or awkwardly. Furthermore, as emphasised earlier, they are essentially of a momentary nature and must usually be followed by a quick return to another fielder or target, which demands judgment of where to send it as well as accuracy of aim.

However, "batting" games present a greater variety not only of activities, but also of roles, than do those of the "net" type, with wicket-keeping or backstopping, in addition to bowling, available to those fielding. There is a further contrast of activity for those fielding close in and those out in the deep field; and in all kinds of game in this category there are opportunities for the fielders to jump, dive and go off-balance, which have such appeal for children, as pointed out in previous pages. Unless, however, the batsmen have a reasonable degree of hitting power the fielders are likely to have little to occupy them and frequently become bored and frustrated.

Activity moreover occurs somewhat sporadically rather than in a continuous fashion, not only because of the very nature of this type of game, with each ball bowled opening a new episode as it were, but also because after some deliveries it is often unnecessary for some of the fielders to go into action at all, and indeed if the batsman is not obliged to run when he does not strike the ball, as in baseball, cricket and stoolball, only the wicket-keeper or backstop may be called upon. ("Tip and Run" is a good example of how children overcome this disadvantage.) This, together with the fact that a player has only one "life" per innings, is a major drawback of "batting" games at the Primary level, if play is according to adult rules, and children understandably tend to lose interest when they are out; they often prefer to join the fielding side and assist their opponents than be consigned to a period of inactivity.

This also illustrates the somewhat individual manner in which these games may be played at an elementary level. Bowler and batsman in particular can function more or less independently; bowling "to a field" (apart from the backstop) is likely to be exceptional, while the only co-operation required between the batsmen is of the sort arising from running between wickets or bases.

Finally, as far as opportunity for invention and variation is concerned, what exercises the ingenuity and imagination of Juniors is less the regulating of the kind of activities involved than the determining of how players may be put out (and in again!), how runs or their equivalent are to be scored (often in conjunction with the latter), and how the various roles of the fielding team are to be changed round. A variety of implements, as well as of the size, composition and weight of the ball, also makes for certain differences in the ultimate nature of the game evolved, and it might be noted here that versions of baseball or softball, in which a two-handed grip on a stick is used, are excellent for Juniors.

Category 3 games

An important feature of "running" games is their potential for continuous activity, activity moreover of the most varied kind since, as originally stated in Chapter 4, players engage in some form of striking or throwing, *and* catching or collecting, *and* carrying or propelling along. There is therefore some complexity on this score alone, especially when a change from one activity to another is made, though the activities differ in difficulty according to whether an implement is used and the actual method of playing the ball.

Striking is usually less problematical for children than in games belonging to either of the other two categories inasmuch as the ball is often already in their possession rather than approaching them; but heading, hitting with a hockey or shinty stick and throwing with a crosse ultimately demand specific skills, and furthermore a final shot at a goal or target is always involved, with the accompanying need for accuracy and force. Catching and collecting, except when an implement is used, are not as chancy as in games of the "batting" kind for the reasons given above and because the ball is almost invariably larger. In any case if it is dropped this is no very serious matter since to despatch it elsewhere is not always essential; but again, hockey- and lacrosse-type games, and to some extent football and rugby, necessitate particular techniques. The simplest form of taking a ball along is to carry it, and bouncing and catching alternately is also relatively easy for Juniors; but dribbling properly with the feet or an implement (that is, as distinct from kicking or hitting the ball some distance and running after it) requires considerable skill, while the netball rule governing the number of steps a player may take when in possession of the ball always renders the official version of this game difficult for children of Primary age.

The range of bodily movement, with the stress on running (usually in a comparatively large space), and with scope also for jumping, as in games of the basketball, football and netball type, has obvious appeal for Juniors, but against all these merits of the *Category 3* games must be set the disadvantages of the numbers involved and the level of co-operation demanded (for these are essentially "passing" games), together with the need to outmanoeuvre opponents with both body and ball. Indeed the opportunity for having an active share in the proceedings at all is largely dependent upon the skill of everyone concerned. Until children have achieved a fair amount of efficiency in the three types of activity which distinguish each game, especially in the methods of propelling the ball along, this kind of game, far from proving exciting and full of action, is often slow and comparatively static or else becomes rather aimless. Sometimes the ball remains in the possession of one incompetent individual who struggles to manoeuvre it or waits uncertainly, not knowing what to do; sometimes an able player keeps it to himself for long periods, or it may be monopolised by just a few, while the rest hang about on the edge of the game, exasperated and probably cold, or converge upon him so that a scrimmage ensues. On other occasions the ball is swung wildly up and down the pitch or court with hardly anyone touching it at all.

In these games there are always several players of both sides on the move simultaneously, so that spatial aspects of play, which are always bound up with precision of timing, are complex. Young children do not easily accommodate to situations in which spaces constantly change in shape and size, the direction of play alters as the ball travels to and fro, and roles keep switching from that of attack to defence or vice versa.

Whereas in games of the "net" or "batting" type a player must move nimbly in order to get to the ball, but once there steadies himself as he proceeds to strike, throw or collect, the fact that in the "running" variety the ball may be retained means that when he is in possession of it he has to continue to use his body in an agile manner to swerve, dodge or out-distance one opponent or more, while at the same time dealing with the ball. When the opposite side is in possession too he must act and think ahead in order to tackle, intercept or make himself easily accessible to his own team-members in readiness for the moment the tide turns.

Tactical play of at least an elementary kind is indispensable in these games and this, as we have seen, calls for a consider-able measure of cognitive and social maturity. Even an appar-ently simple "passing" game of two-a-side is quite advanced since each player is related differently to each of the rest of the group—to his partner, both as a sender and receiver of the ball, to his own "man" whom he must guard in defence and from whom he must free himself when on the attack, and to his opponent's partner, whose relative position to each of the others he must watch carefully in order both to assist his own ally and to mark his opponent effectively. Several players a side obviously complicate the situation yet further, and the understanding of particular functions of individuals within a team becomes necessary. The role of the goalkeeper in games of the football or hockey type obviously involves special responsibilities requiring separate attention.

It is not surprising that the modifications of games belonging to *Category 3* which children introduce are usually first and foremost to do with the numbers of players, which tends to simplify all four aspects of play—physical (not so much dodging and manoeuvring required), cognitive (fewer stratagems called for), social (co-operation reduced and roles not so clearly defined, players able to share equally in attack and defence) and moral (less legislation needed, particularly as regards positional play). They may well be unaware of course that these are modifications of the original version at all, but tend perhaps to be strongly influenced by adult methods of actually playing the ball, and may need to be encouraged to be less conservative and more imaginative in this matter.

It seems a pity, for instance, that something in the nature of a mixture of netball and basketball, or football and rugby, or with elements of all four, should not be played. In fact probably one of the easiest kinds of "running" games for Juniors is one in which throwing (including the "sling" type of throw) and/or kicking and heading is the means of sending the ball; catching and collecting with hands, or with hands and feet, the means of gaining possession; and carrying and/or bouncing the means of propelling it along.

Children can also be helped to devise a variety of methods of beginning play and of re-starting it after a goal has been scored and when it goes outside the playing area; to determine what constitutes fair means of obtaining the ball; to settle ways of shooting goals and what privileges, if any, are to be extended to the goalkeeper; to decide on boundaries and any limitations of areas to particular players; and to

make provision for dealing with such eventualities as obstruct-
ion, offside and so on.

A greater range of equipment than that usually considered
adequate for these games is also desirable, both in respect of
the balls and implements used, and also as regards goals and
nets. These last seem always to be either small, circular, high
and horizontal to the ground, or large and rectangular with
ground level included. There is surely scope here for improvis-
ation of apparatus (as well as invention on the part of manufacturers) which would permit rings or targets of other shapes
to be tilted, and goals between uprights to be divided horizontally, to be higher than they are wide, and square as well as
oblong. A stick or bat which could be used with one hand
would promote a further variety of "running" game in which
striking, patting upwards and bouncing would become the
three activities involved, or, if designed so as to hold a ball,
could lead to throwing, catching and carrying respectively;
nor is it impossible to imagine games in which hoops or
quoits instead of balls are used, or for that matter moving
targets.

To sum up. It appears that the simplest kind of game for
children is either one of the "net" sort in which a fairly large
ball is used, but no implement, and in which the number per
side is anything from one to five; or a hybrid variety of the
"running" type as described above, also for small numbers
and with a reasonably-sized goal-mouth but on a small
pitch. At the opposite extreme, and most difficult for Juniors,
are those in *Category 3* in which a small ball and an implement are used, the playing area is large (since this requires
considerable hitting power) and numbers exceed, say, five a
side.

This is not to imply that hockey-, shinty- and lacrosse-type
games are totally unsuitable for children of Primary age. Indeed
there seems no good educational reason why they have become the prerogative of the Secondary stage or reserved for
the fourth year of the Junior school. But it is essential that
numbers, equipment, and size of pitch are appropriate for
the children concerned, and the teacher must obviously know,

not so much the rules of the official versions of these games, but how to assist girls and boys to acquire experience in the fundamental activities involved. These deserve more detailed consideration, particularly by teachers of older Juniors and beyond, and this is the subject of the next chapter.

CHAPTER 6

Analysis of Games Activities

If we now return to the three basic activities of sending away, gaining possession of, and travelling with an object, and further examine these, a number of fundamentals underlying each becomes apparent whatever the nature of the object and the means of controlling it.

The discussion which follows is by no means exhaustive, and for the teacher requiring further technical details there is ample information available in books on specific games. With young children, as also at first with exceptionally gifted players, it is neither necessary nor desirable for them to think analytically—indeed, it may prove inhibiting to their freedom of action and personal style if demanded too early; but for older ones, and also for the teacher, it is essential to appreciate what makes for skilled performance and to be able to pinpoint the distinctive features of any process so that specific weaknesses be detected. In general what is needed is an emphasis within the general flow of action rather than a taking to pieces of the whole and a practising of separate parts. Primary children are often keen and competent observers and should be helped to develop this ability in the games lesson in order both to learn themselves and to assist others (as is already common practice in dance and gymnastics). It also seems desirable that, wherever appropriate, their interest in and curiosity about why and how things happen should be stimulated and satisfied, and that what they learn in one situation be related to others relevantly similar.

Striking and throwing

Whatever the size and shape of an object, and whether it is struck or thrown by a part of the body or an implement, its ultimate behaviour is largely governed by:

(a) the preparation;

(b) the timing of contact or release;

(c) the transference of weight and follow-through.

Particular considerations arise in connection with the differing *grips* on a ball and on an implement, and the fact that in hitting a ball in games of the "batting" type the batsman takes up a *stance* as he awaits delivery. These points will be referred to later.

Whether an object is struck by a racket, a bat or stick, or thrown from the hands or a crosse, the fact that it is *sent away* from the player usually demands a lift or swing in *preparation*, a *main action* in which the weight is transferred as contact or release is effected, and a *follow-through* which may include further steps.

1. Preparation

Although there are no preliminaries to the main action in the case of a ball being scooped up and sent underarm all in one movement, and in certain strokes such as the push or flick in hockey, in general a stroke or throw is preceded by a lift or swing, however small, into the opposite direction to that into which the object is aimed.

In the majority of instances (and in all cases in games of the "net" type), the object is struck or thrown into an area in front of the player, and the preparation is a sideways or backward movement. In hitting and kicking the preparatory action determines the part of the implement or foot which makes contact with the object, so influencing its direction and trajectory. But in most hitting and overarm throwing actions the preparation necessitates also a twist of the upper part of the body (this happens too when a ball is kicked so as to make it swerve), and a taking of the weight away from the zone into which the object is to be directed. The extent to which this twist occurs, as well as the size of the swing or lift, contributes to the amount of force exerted, but this also depends on other factors, including the fluency with which the preparation merges into the main action.

Although in many ways a stroke or throw should be regarded as a single action rather than consisting of several parts, it can be useful for the experienced striker to check this fluency when at the last minute he changes his mind about the placing and power of his shot. In any event it is helpful to recognise the rhythm of the total action, with the preparation generally less stressed and of shorter duration than the main action, and to appreciate that the force, rhythm and pathway of the movement are interdependent.

2. Main action

In all forms of striking and throwing the timing of contact or release is of considerable importance, and the direction and flight of the object are partly determined by whether it is hit or thrown "early" or "late". These terms refer, in throwing, to the moment of release in relation to the arm action (that is, whether the ball is thrown or bowled when the forward action has just begun or held until later during this action), and in striking, to the position of the ball or shuttle relative to the body as contact is made (that is, whether it is struck in front of, at the side of or slightly behind the body). It is of course more difficult to gauge when to hit an oncoming object than one already under control. The former demands judging the trajectory and speed at which it is travelling through the air or off the ground and the positioning accordingly of the player himself; in the latter instance he has more chance of steering the ball to an appropriate distance and place and of choosing the moment of striking.

The synchronising of the main action with the transference of weight is a different aspect of timing but nevertheless of importance, and in the case of overarm bowling is one of the more complex features of co-ordination. Where twisting of the body occurs, the untwisting into the opposite direction also coincides with the transference of weight and the actual stroke or throw; where a player has turned sideways on to the ball without twisting, the shoulders and upper part of the trunk are often turned towards the direction of the aim as the forward action begins—indeed an action of the arm may be initiated by the trunk, and is especially important for players lacking relatively strong wrists or shoulders.

The transference of weight itself is usually from the back foot to the front, and if the weight of the body is used to advantage several steps forward will probably follow. Both in the preparation to strike an object, and at the moment of contact, it is vital for the inexperienced player to watch it all the time[23] and to lift his head only after impact. Whether his weight is applied under, over or behind the object largely determines whether it is lofted, directed onto the ground or sent along or parallel to it. If a player is forced onto the "wrong" foot in those games in which he faces an oncoming object he may, according to his experience, attempt to compensate for the lack of weight in the stroke by an extraforceful wrist action, but sometimes, especially in games of the "batting" type, he deliberately or instinctively plays off the back foot and can in so doing "lean" on the ball and still use the weight of his body.

3. Follow-through

As the ball, quoit or shuttle is struck or thrown, the arm or leg action continues in the direction into which the object has been sent, and may eventually sweep round across the player's body. This follow-through is dependent on the nature of the stroke or throw, particularly on the force applied and the angle of the implement or part of the body used at the moment of impact or release. A full-blooded action will, of course, result in a free, flourishing conclusion; after a delicate or checked shot it will be correspondingly slight or even prevented altogether, as for example in a stop-volley in tennis.

Attention to the pathway and fluency of the follow-through can contribute to the accuracy of aim which, as emphasised in Chapter 4, is the main purpose of striking and throwing. This may be seen to depend on all three aspects—preparation, main action and follow-through—since these are in reality inseparable from one another, but concentration on one part may assist the skilful execution of the whole.

Although, as previously stated, striking and throwing are activities complete in themselves, a player must always prepare immediately afterwards, or even during the action itself, for his next move, and after his follow-through he must usually re-position himself or set off for a base or post. This might be termed a "strategic" action as distinct from the kind which has a direct influence on the object.

4. Stance

The positioning of the body in relation to the ball or shuttle has been emphasised as of major importance in the timing of any shot, but when a batsman awaits the delivery of a ball from a bowler, as in all the "batting" games, there are somewhat different points to be taken into account. Since he is not concerned with running towards it, and then possibly turning and/or twisting his body as he prepares to kick or hit, he is able to adopt a stance which is already balanced and more or less sideways on to the approaching ball.

Nevertheless, as in all instances in which an oncoming object is to be hit, less time is available for judging the kind of stroke required, and whereas in throwing or in striking a ball already under control there is only one main consideration (the direction into which it shall be aimed), there is now the additional one of estimating its speed and trajectory, and possibly its behaviour after bouncing. The waiting batsman therefore needs to be able quickly to transfer his weight onto either foot, or indeed to take several steps, and must closely watch the bowler's run-up, bowling action and finally the ball itself. His initial stance will consequently be with the weight equally distributed directly over the balls of the feet and with a slight "give" in the knees.

5. Grip

When a racket, bat or stick is used, the question arises as to how to hold it effectively. Whether one hand is employed or two, the grip must be such that the implement is felt to be, and can be used as, an extension of the arm or arms. It must also be capable of being easily adjusted, as is necessary for instance in preparation for a backhand shot in tennis after a forehand, or for a drive following dribbling in hockey. The distance between the hands in the case of a two-handed grip should never be so great as to prevent the *upper* from imparting force and guidance to the stroke.

The grip on a ball is also of some importance, especially, of course, when it is to be bowled. Although the total arm action and that of the trunk are different in one- and two-handed throws, the fingers always play a decisive part in influencing the direction of the ball, and give additional impetus to it as it is finally released. In all one-handed throws the way they are placed around it, together with their action as it leaves the hand, helps to determine its spin and trajectory.

It is important to note that, while kicking and hitting a ball with the hand(s) are relatively easy, striking with an implement, particularly when an oncoming object is involved, demands considerable co-ordination and is always a more complex process than throwing.

Catching and collecting

When gaining possession is considered in detail it is worth noting that since all varieties are essentially of a momentary nature a good deal more than the action itself is usually involved.

1. Preparation
Before being able to catch a ball or quoit with one hand or two, trap with the feet, receive with a crosse or field on a hockey stick, a player must first concentrate on the development of those situations which may lead to his gaining possession, as well as on the object itself, and be prepared to move into an appropriate position in order to receive it safely. Ultimate success depends both on the ability to get to the right place at the right time and, once there, to control the ball or quoit effectively.

As already pointed out in Chapter 4, in games of the "batting" type the flight of the ball is difficult for any but an experienced player to predict, and for the close-in fielder this necessitates a stance which is balanced, yet not static, so that swift action is possible; the knees should be flexed, the weight over the balls of the feet, and the head and hands steady. Anticipation of the need to move depends upon this state of alertness and the concentration mentioned above, and enables the player to leap, dive or lunge if only fractionally before the ball reaches him. The deep fieldsman, however, like the goalkeeper in football or hockey, seeks to maintain a state of readiness by ranging over an area rather than staying on one spot, and as the bowler prepares to deliver the ball already begins to move in towards the batsman.

In games involving passing between players the receiver can anticipate more accurately when and where he is likely to be sent the ball and, indeed, has the responsibility of facilitating this by moving into a position where he can easily gain possession, or by creating a space into which he can run "onto" it. The skilful player often starts to make the decisive move, in fact, even before his team-mate who will strike or throw the ball to him has himself obtained it and, since he may also have to free himself from an opponent marking him, the timing of the moment when, for example, he makes his sprint or changes direction is vital. He can also assist the accuracy of the pass by indicating precisely where he wants the ball—in hockey, for instance, the blade of the stick can present a target; in netball, the outstretched hand.

Thus there are similar factors to be taken into account in catching or collecting as in striking an oncoming ball, especially when it is in the air, and the judging of its *direction, trajectory* and *speed* is essential, as well as the *positioning of the body* in relation to it. In general the receiver aims to get in line with the ball as it approaches him, but his actual positioning immediately before contact will vary according to how it is travelling, and whether he is collecting it with his hands or an implement. If it is dropping from above he needs to be almost directly beneath it, if rolling along the ground or bouncing up, behind but slightly to one side in order that the ensuing throw, hit or further manoeuvring of it can proceed without delay. (This will be to the left in the case of a right-handed thrower, to the right for a left-hander; in hockey, of course, he usually tries to be to the left, except for the reverse hit.) Collecting a ball with the hands as it travels along the ground, whether the fielder meets it, cuts it off at an angle or pursues it (*see* Chapter 4), demands also a quick crouching action as the player pounces upon it.

To sum up, powers of anticipation and quick reaction, nimble footwork and general bodily agility are of prime importance in preparing to catch or collect a ball or quoit. It now remains to consider details of the actions involved.

2. Main action

Collecting a quoit or small ball is a grasping action, and though for the latter the hands may be cupped in readiness, they fasten round the ball in a manner similar to that of gripping a quoit; other kinds of collecting are "gathering" actions which bring the ball under control in a somewhat different way. Since, however, gaining possession involves the *drawing in* of the object towards the body, the preparation and recovery, whether with a hand, foot or an implement, are determined by similar considerations.

In all cases the *preparation* necessitates reaching towards the object, with the attention focused wholly upon it, and the part of the body or implement appropriately angled. Also the weight is shifted into this direction (and may include a jump), although it may almost immediately be transferred as contact is made. Often there is one step or more into the opposite direction which, together with the relaxed "give" of the hands, stick or body, absorbs the shock of impact. In most cases this *recovery* either fuses into the preparation for the next action (the backswing for throwing or hitting), or is converted into a new activity such as carrying or propelling.

While, therefore, after striking or throwing what has been called a "strategic" action is called for, in catching and collecting there is, in addition, a new activity to be initiated, and in several games of the "running" type a decision must be made as to whether to despatch the ball at once or retain possession for a time.

Carrying and propelling

The chief requirements of these in relation to a ball are to keep it under control while on the run, and to manoeuvre it in such a way both so as to prevent an opponent from gaining possession of it and so that it may easily be struck or thrown at an appropriate moment.

In games such as basketball, netball and rugby, in which no implement is used, the freedom to move is hampered very little by the fact that the ball is carried or propelled by the hands, and the direction of steps is easily varied. When two hands are used the normal action of the arms may be somewhat restricted, and in a game such as rugby it can be an advantage to have a free arm to assist in sprinting, as well as to hand off opponents. In lacrosse, which involves the specialised technique of cradling, the loss of speed is negligible once this has been mastered.

When the feet are used to propel the ball along they have of course a dual function, and travelling is not quite as simple as when they are free for this purpose alone, as in the instances above. Yet further complications arise when an implement such as a hockey or shinty stick is used to dribble the ball, and since once contact is made it is maintained, carrying is always less difficult than propelling.

Whenever contact is intermittent (*see* Chapter 4) the ball should not be allowed to run so far ahead of the player that he loses control of it, nor so close that he cannot progress at speed, but kept just sufficiently far away to permit him to continue using his feet freely and nimbly. In the case of hockey the position of the stick relative to the body, as well as that of the body to the ball, is important, and the grip on it is usually a modified version of that used for a drive.

Games which involve travelling with the ball are also those in which passing and tackling are a feature (an exception to the latter is netball), and when carrying or propelling, a player must be prepared both to dodge while retaining possession of the ball, and to change from this activity to hitting, kicking or throwing as the case may be. Skill in outmanoeuvring opponents demands bodily agility and good ball control in games in which propelling occurs, and in these a further difficulty is presented by the fact that the attention is directed downward, thus necessitating a constant change of focus. Watch must be kept on the positions of other players as well as on the ball itself, and the decision to pass is therefore more difficult than during carrying, since in these circumstances a player can throw without first looking at the ball.

Similarly, to change from carrying to throwing is easy, as also is that from dribbling to striking with the feet, but when a stick is used this is rather more difficult as the position of the body in relation to the ball may have to be adjusted; a push or flick, however, does not require either.

As mentioned at the end of Chapter 4, implements as well as balls are carried, and since this may be a feature of games of all three types it merits attention. The importance of a racket, stick or bat being held so that it is felt to be an extension of the body has already been stressed in connection with striking, but this applies too when the player is not engaged in actually manoeuvring the ball or making a stroke. In "net" and "running" games he must be able quickly and easily to adjust his implement into positions of readiness while he is on the move, so that the ultimate stroke may be made effectively. In "batting" games the same is true when the striker runs between posts or wickets and uses his stick or bat in an attempt to extend his reach when contacting base or crease.

An understanding of the various aspects of the three basic activities is helpful to the teacher in his planning of a games programme. In addition he needs to consider them from the point of view of the children themselves, and the next chapter is devoted to an examination of their achievements and problems in relation to each, and of means whereby comprehensive and progressive experience may be ensured.

Notes

23. It is important to try to do this even though it is impossible at the actual moment of impact.

CHAPTER 7

Lesson Material

Striking and throwing

From our knowledge of children and the analysis of games activities given in the previous chapters it becomes apparent that the kind of striking action which they find most easy is kicking, while the most difficult is that of hitting an oncoming object with an implement, especially one with a long handle and a narrow striking surface. As for their capacity to throw, even before they can walk young children show enjoyment of dropping and releasing things, and of combining this with pushing them away, which is, after all, the basis of a throwing action. However, for some time they have little control over direction or distance, since to time the moment to let go and to judge the amount of force required, let alone to aim, is a complex business. Kicking, however, demands no such releasing action, though it necessitates, of course, the co-ordination essential to balancing on one foot.

Whether throwing a fairly large ball with two hands or managing a small ball with one, children employ initially a similar type of action, the hands being placed underneath the ball so that it is sent upwards, and the arms as a whole being used, with the palms rather than the fingers giving the final push; they also often hold on to it so long as to cause it to disappear over their heads.

When they attempt to throw overarm there is often a certain awkwardness in the transition between the backward movement and the main action as they pause with the ball

66

behind the head, and two separate actions occur instead of a fluent merging of one with the other. Moreover, as they project it forward they tend to use the forearm only, with little participation by the shoulder, wrist or fingers; and because they usually take up a stance facing squarely forward, as when throwing underarm, there is no twisting of the body or transference of weight, and consequently the ball does not travel very far.

Kicking entails less complexity of co-ordination, especially from a stationary position. A child can continue to face the direction of his shot all the time, and if he takes a run at it he can approach it in a direct line and shoot his foot straight forward almost as an extension of his running action; the preliminary backswing of the leg occurs quite naturally, merging without a break into the forward thrust. It is often more satisfying for children to kick a ball than to throw one, for by this means they can usually send it further.

If we recall the young child's enjoyment of the sensation of movement for its own sake we shall not be surprised to find that, in his exploratory play with bats and balls, skill in controlling them is not always the primary concern (especially if he is denied sufficient opportunities to satisfy his need for bodily action in dance and on agility apparatus). At the Infant stage many children, if they use a ball in a "games-like" way at all (see page 27), seem to delight in throwing it wildly into the air, or taking a full-blooded swing at it with bat or hand, rather than keeping it near to them and practising.

However, when they do begin to settle to acquiring more specific skill in actually handling small apparatus, rather than attempting to deal with an oncoming ball or shuttle they usually spend a considerable amount of time in throwing balls and striking them not only with a bat but also with the hands, including bouncing them and patting them upwards or against a wall, either continuously or alternately hitting them and letting them drop to the ground. These tend to be comparatively static activities at first but, with increased bodily mastery and manipulative dexterity, children become more nimble on their feet and able to adjust more readily not only to the sometimes unexpected behaviour of a ball, but also to the unpredictable flight of a shuttle (which always necessitates a certain quickness and agility in order for it to be kept continuously airborne), and to keep them in play for longer periods.

Striking objects in the air often develops from bouncing or tossing them up a little way (or almost placing them on the bat) with one hand and hitting at them with the other, and this is obviously easier than attempting to hit a ball that is sent to them by someone else. It is not only the judgment of its trajectory and speed which presents difficulties, and perhaps too the way in which it bounces up off the ground, but also, as in throwing, the transition between the preparatory backswing and the main action. In "batting" games, in which a preliminary stance is adopted, the backswing tends to become "frozen" into a held position or even eliminated altogether, with the bat or stick merely stuck or "hung" out. In "net" games there is the additional problem of moving into an appropriate position in relation to the ball or shuttle after getting to the required place at the right time, and then making the actual stroke. Somewhat similar problems arise in connection with heading, an absence of an adequate preparatory movement downward being particularly common; but the action itself is less complex on the whole than hitting with an implement, and once the correct part of the head is used and the importance of watching and meeting the ball is appreciated, girls as well as boys can effectively employ this method of striking.

It is interesting to note that children may in fact pick up and handle with *two* hands an implement which the adult may assume should always be used with only one; sometimes, moreover, the right hand is placed above the left, even in the case of otherwise right-handed players, especially when they first experiment with long-handled sticks. Cross-batting a ball, that is, sweeping it horizontally across the body, also seems much more natural to many children than following the pathways of the orthodox strokes and drives of the major games.

When they grip a racket or stick with one hand they are apt to hold it too far away from the end of the handle to be able to use it freely, and also to place the fingers too far round to the right (in the case of right-handed players), so that they hit always underneath the object, with the elbow cramped against the side of the body. Placing the index finger along, instead of round, implements of all kinds is common too and may, of course, be dangerous. Difficulties with grip, it may be noted, are often due to the fact that children's wrists and shoulders are relatively weak in relation to the implements they have at their disposal, which may be large and heavy with handles that are both too long and too thick. If there is an adequate selection they sometimes need guidance in choosing one of the appropriate size and weight, as they are apt to imagine that the bigger the better!

In all methods of sending away an object, except by heading, there are three common features which children appear to find quite difficult—to concentrate on the target until after the ball has left the hand(s) in the case of throwing and, in that of striking, on the ball or shuttle itself until after impact;[24] to synchronise the transference of weight with the main arm or leg action and to use the trunk effectively in order to get power into the main action; and to follow through freely with arms and feet after releasing or striking the object. Often after taking one step forward they are prone to step back again rather than go on, and since in all games there is always the need after sending away for a "strategic" action demanding several steps (*see* page 60), they should be helped to discover the importance of continuing to move on as the follow-through is completed.

When, however, children do acquire the knack of overarm throwing, of one- and two-handed hitting and of other forms of striking, it is noticeable that they often have a fluency of action and a harmony of movement, especially between the right and left sides of the body and between the upper and lower half, which might well be the envy of many adults. Delight in the sensation of movement in activities of a primarily functional nature is hardly to be distinguished among children from that involved in the use of the body in an expressive way, and in the games situation the various methods of sending away an object seem in particular to be enjoyed as actions in themselves, irrespective of their results.

The abandon and forcefulness of thumping or flinging a ball, no matter where it goes, is a source of pleasure to many children not only when they are very young, but throughout their Primary years. Interest in aiming is something which, though developing gradually and arising from the special satisfaction of achieving exactly the right direction, timing and force, seems to be secondary to the zest for physical action.[25]

The unorthodox techniques which children often employ in striking and throwing, especially in respect of gripping and making strokes with implements, sometimes give the teacher who is knowledgeable in these matters cause for concern. He may well be torn between a strong desire to show them the correct methods from the very beginning and so prevent bad habits from becoming ingrained, and allowing sufficient opportunity for exploration and the development of an individual style. In general it would seem that children are likely to suffer more from coaching at too early an age than from a certain healthy "neglect". Adequate time to experiment with an implement and to become thoroughly familiar with it so that it is felt as an extension of the arm and not as a foreign object attached to the hand, is essential, and in the long run usually proves to have been well spent. Similarly it is often of little avail to try to teach young children how to throw overarm; the "do it this way" method has certain limitations.

It is obviously most important that opportunities for all kinds of striking and throwing are given at the Primary level since, as we have already seen (Chapter 2), these activities are of the kind which give rise to games of the type under discussion, and are basic to any game as originally defined. In seeking to ensure all-round experience in this respect the teacher may find the following synopsis useful.

1. Varieties of "sending away"

(a) *Striking.* Opportunities are desirable for both girls and boys to participate in activities involving heading, kicking and one- and two-handed hitting with a variety of implements over short and long distances. Head, feet and hands are those most usual for controlling games apparatus, and children should be helped to discover the appropriateness of particular parts of these. They find fists, for example, an effective means of sending fairly large balls some distance, but in games of the volley-ball type they may also find elbows and shoulders useful for keeping the ball aloft in an emergency.

(b) *Throwing.* This includes rolling, under- and over-arm bowling,[26] throwing quoits or balls over short and long distances and throwing from a crosse.

2. Apparatus[27]

(a) *Objects.* Ideally quoits and shuttles as well as a good range of balls should be provided. Airflow balls behave very differently when hit from, for instance, the heavier, more resilient kind, and table-tennis balls are useful with light bats indoors, especially for Infants. If funds are limited it is probably better to have a few of several kinds than to try to provide each child in the class with one of the same sort. An exception might be playballs, which, in any case, are amongst the cheapest.

(b) *Implements.* Again a good assortment is desirable and, as with balls, it would seem wiser to have a few bats and sticks of various kinds rather than a large quantity of only one or two. For most Infants, lightweight bats with relatively large hitting surfaces and short handles that are comfortable to grip are preferable to the long-handled variety with a small surface, and are useful too for lower Juniors. Sticks as well as bats suitable for two-handed use should be included if possible.

3. Practice situations

When children reach the stage of needing to practise specific aspects of striking and throwing arising from their games and games activities, it can be useful to find ways of improving accuracy from different angles and distances, and the following types of *aiming* might be considered.

(a) *Aiming at fixed targets.* That is:

(i) areas on ground level such as hoops on the floor, chalked circles, skittles and wickets, so that *aiming is downward* and can include overarm bowling;

(ii) areas of varied size on a wall and targets such as

stoolball bases, so that aiming is more or less *parallel to the ground* and can include underarm bowling;

(*iii*) rings such as those on netball posts (which should be adjustable to various heights), so that aiming is *upwards;*

(*iv*) goals between upright posts of various heights and widths so that aiming can vary. The use of all parts of such goals should be encouraged, except in cases where it is dangerous to loft the ball.

Fixed targets which are also guarded increase the degree of skill required and of course present a situation nearer to that of an actual game.

(*b*) *Aiming at moving targets.* That is:

(*i*) players in the vicinity of a base, post or wickets who are seeking to put out batsmen and who need a throw directed through the air or on the bounce;

(*ii*) players who are running at speed and who require a pass directed into their hands or at their feet, or stick, or into a space so that they can run "onto" the ball;

(*iii*) moving objects or players. Though not typical of major games there seems no reason why these should not be included, always provided, of course, that there is no danger involved.

In addition to those given above, situations which provide for striking in front of a wicket or post and hitting over a net can be included. In the former the batsman not only needs to defend the target but may also try to place his shots in a variety of directions in relation to it, that is, behind, square on and to the right and left in front of it. In the latter a continuous stream of balls sent "sympathetically" from the other side of the net again makes it possible for the player to concentrate on *where* he tries to send the ball, and also draws attention to the need constantly to re-position after every shot.

It is worth mentioning again in this connection that most young children, as well as those interested in pursuing skill as a means to an end, enjoy co-operating with others on similar principles to those just instanced, and may therefore be encouraged to find methods such as rolling, bouncing and throwing a ball underarm to a striker so that it is at first easy to hit and then progressively more difficult.

Catching and collecting

Grasping objects and drawing them towards the body are, like releasing and pushing away, activities in which children engage from the time they are babies, but to catch something that is in motion, especially if it is approaching directly through the air, and to hold on to it, demands (as explained in Chapter 6) a great deal more than the grasping and gathering action itself. It was stated then that powers of anticipation and quick reaction, nimble footwork and general bodily agility are of prime importance in preparing to catch a ball or quoit, and these powers are, of course, far from well developed when children first come to school.

In games activities they have greater difficulty in gaining possession than in sending away, not only at Infant level but during the Junior stage too. The concentration and forethought needed to sum up the development of situations which are likely to lead to their being called upon to receive a ball, whether from a pass or when they are fielding, are often beyond them, as is also the ability to judge accurately its direction, trajectory and speed; and even if they do manage to get into an appropriate position at an opportune moment, they often miss it altogether or touch it but again lose contact with it. This is due to difficulties of co-ordination on the one hand, and on the other of controlling going and stopping. Adroit management of the feet may be required in taking a catch with the hands, as in hitting an oncoming ball in "net" and "batting" games, so that running is momentarily checked immediately before contact is effected; collecting, by contrast, often necessitates keeping on the move.

Many young children's first experience of catching is when a well-meaning adult or older child sends them a ball from a short distance, and it is obviously easier in such circumstances if the ball is fairly large and if two hands rather than one are used. Collecting a small one that is rolling along the ground by grabbing it from above with one hand, however, appears to be almost as easy, for although the moment to reach down for it must be accurately timed, this sudden crouching action is not unfamiliar to a young child with his relatively short legs and tendency to assume squatting positions (and is certainly less difficult from this point of view than for the adult). Success in picking up a ball that is rolling away from him seems to precede success in other forms of catching and collecting, probably because the ball is losing speed, and also because lack of dexterity in catching leads to plenty of practice in retrieving objects in this way! When a ball is rolling towards him, however, he eventually needs to learn the disadvantages of grasping it from above.

The active nature of the skill involved in catching and collecting a ball or quoit, which led to our adoption of the term "gaining possession" to describe the various forms it was designed to cover, is well illustrated by young children's actions of seizing a rolling ball, but is precisely what is lacking when they try to catch with hands, or later with an implement. These tend to be stuck out rather passively, though often stiffly, so that the ball bounces out of or off them, and there is usually no action of gathering in towards the body.

Beanbags (or bags of sawdust, rubber chippings or other types of filling) can serve a useful purpose in the early stages from this point of view, since the children's fingers can dig into the material and a real grasp can be achieved. As beanbags go "dead" when dropped, this also can be of advantage in comparison with balls, especially in circumstances where rolling down slopes, through railings and into other inaccessible or dangerous places is likely to occur. They do not, however, in any way replace balls, and their uses for games of the kind under discussion are somewhat limited.

Skill in catching develops very much in conjunction with throwing and/or bouncing during individual play, and tossing and catching objects, whether pebbles, balls or quoits, are conveniently paired activities. Much time is often spent by children at the Infant and Junior level with a ball against a wall, and when this involves throwing it is usually an indication that catching as well as throwing has become of interest.

As in the sending away of an object, fluency in the whole process of catching or collecting is achieved only gradually, the preparatory movement of reaching towards it, like that of the backswing in striking and throwing, not at first merging fluently into the main action. This happens less when they catch a quoit which is clutched at rather than waited for, though of course the fact that once again it approaches through the air and spins in a variety of ways *en route* makes for certain problems. Children, however, usually enjoy the challenge of something which behaves quite differently from a ball, and when in particular it travels in the sagittal plane (like a wheel bowling along) it is not much more difficult to grasp.

As already indicated, fielding on a hockey stick, catching in a crosse and trapping with the feet eventually require specific techniques, but in hockey there may at least be some advantage in the fact that the ball approaches along the ground and is also, as a result, slowing down somewhat. This may happen too in the case of trapping, and if the ball is bouncing up off the ground it is possible also to use the chest and front of the body. Whenever a ball travels towards them there is a tendency for children to wait for it to arrive rather than going to meet it and, with a stick, to put it down too late instead of keeping it close to the ground.

The most difficult situation of all, as far as gaining possession of an object is concerned, is that occurring in "batting" games when a ball glances off the striker's stick or bat, especially if the fielder is at fairly close range. Not only, as we have seen, is it almost impossible for him to pre-judge the direction, level and speed, but the fact that he never knows when to expect it, particularly if coupled with a certain keenness to put the batsman out, or at least prevent him from scoring, is apt to cause a division of his attention which easily leads to misfielding.

The momentary nature of all forms of collecting and catching has already been stressed and it is understandable that for some time, having achieved a measure of success in actually gaining possession of a ball or quoit, children are comparatively unable to exploit this to advantage because they hesitate before initiating a new activity. Even when they are accustomed to making appropriate decisions during the act of gathering itself as to where to send the ball (as in "batting" games), or what to do with it, that is, pass or retain possession of it (as in "running" games), they may lack skill not only in promptly changing their focus and aiming accurately, but also in fusing the recovery phase of receiving into the backswing of a throwing or hitting action, or in adjusting quickly to propelling or carrying the ball along.

When children field a ball coming along the ground towards them with hands or a stick, this delay is often because they approach it directly from behind, and so have to make a major bodily adjustment in order to re-position for the throw or hit. Although the feet may form a second line of defence in the first instance, players should be encouraged to discover the advantages of crouching down to one side of the ball with that foot in front which is the opposite of the throwing arm. In hockey or shinty it should be easy for them to appreciate why the feet should be to the left of the ball.

Children's success therefore in each kind of "gaining possession" as a whole process depends on a number of interrelated factors, and their capacity to judge what to do *before* and immediately *after* the moment of contact is as important as the moment itself.

Since "gaining possession" is essential in all kinds of fielding and passing and also constitutes an important part of any "net" game in which a quoit is used, a variety of experience in the different forms of catching and collecting should be made available to girls and boys alike and will, of course, often be part of activities in which they or others strike or throw a ball or quoit.

1. Varieties of "gaining possession"

(a) Catching. It will be recalled that throughout this book this term has been used to distinguish those activities in which an object is taken in the air from those in which it is collected as it travels along the ground. This aspect of receiving therefore chiefly involves the use of one hand or two, as well as lacrosse sticks, and it is not outside the bounds of possibility that with rounders sticks among equipment to choose from children will invent games in which these are

used to catch quoits by "spearing" them, as they sometimes also do with their arms.

(b) *Collecting.* This includes the use of hands, trapping with the feet and fielding with hockey, shinty and lacrosse sticks, and children need opportunities for gaining skill in all these varieties, and for discovering basic similarities and specific differences between them.

2. Apparatus[28]

In addition to beanbags, quoits and balls of varying size, shape, composition and weight, valuable pieces of equipment for catching practice which provide a variety of trajectory are cradles and adjustable slip-catchers. A wall, of course, or rough piece of ground, is always a useful aid in this respect.

3. Practice situations

Exploration, experiment and practice may be of three types:

(a) *Individual activity.* Catching and collecting from one's own throwing, patting, bouncing, rolling, kicking and hitting activities are often incidental to the main interest of "sending away" but may, obviously, become the major concern.

(b) *Co-operative paired activity.*

(i) Another person aims directly into the hands or at the feet or stick of the receiver, so that the ball or quoit on reaching him is:

dropping;
rising;
travelling parallel to the ground; or
travelling smoothly or bouncing along the ground.

In all these instances the receiver may start from a stationary position (in which case he can concentrate wholly on watching the object), or already be on the move.

(ii) Another person sends the object:

so that it falls short;
so that the receiver has to jump;
so that he has to chase it or retrieve on the run;
to his right and left from in front;
to his right and left from behind;
into a space so that he runs "onto" it.

(c) Competitive group activity. A player A:

> *(i)* marks an opponent B, or marks the space, while another, C, attempts to pass to B, so that he has to dodge in order to free himself or create a space into which he can move as the pass is made;
>
> *(ii)* aims at a goal or area which an opponent is guarding;
>
> *(iii)* aims to pass to another player whom an opponent tries to prevent from gaining possession of the ball;
>
> *(iv)* is bowled a ball while a receiver waits behind in the role of wicketkeeper or backstop.

In situations *(b)* and *(c)* the activity can be combined with further action in the form of sending the object to a particular target, or propelling or carrying it along.

Carrying and propelling

To run along bowling a hoop or kicking a stone or can is a favourite occupation of long standing among children of a variety of ages. Often the object tends to be struck and then pursued rather than being closely controlled while in motion, but there is an essential difference between this type of activity in which they try to steer something as they run, and that in which they simply throw, hit or kick it as, for example, when they aim a pebble at a stump, or toss a stone into the air and strike at it with a stick.

The chief feature of those activities which have been termed "carrying" and "propelling" in this book is that the player keeps on the move while retaining the ball in his possession for short or longer periods, either by continuous or by intermittent contact. In those games in which this happens (all belonging to Category 3) it is a prime means of getting the ball into the opponents' territory and near enough to their goal in order to be able to shoot. As already emphasised, both speed and adaptability are called for and, while these are necessary in all games, they are at a premium in those in which taking the ball along occurs. It is not surprising, therefore, that Infants do not readily engage in these activities, and that when they do, genuine propelling is infrequent.

In striking, catching and collecting, some of the difficulties which children encounter are, as we have seen, the subtle transferences of weight, the abrupt halts and the rapid dashes which may be demanded; but at least sprinting a relatively long distance without interruption is comparatively easy. In itself the sheer act of running is a source of great delight to many children, even when they are very young and rather unsteady on their feet; but in conjunction with the manoeuvring of an object, especially by means of an implement, it becomes a complex operation, and a considerable degree of skill is involved in the various kinds of travelling with a ball which are possible in games.

If contact is continuous there are few problems, and carrying the ball while on the run is one of the simplest methods of dealing with it that children find; but in the early stages their ability to weave in and out of other players while keeping control of it is limited, and the usual means of outplaying opponents is simply superior speed. Holding a ball in one hand so as to leave the other arm free to assist sprinting has obviously an advantage over using two, and is easiest with an oval ball; provided that it is not too large for the pointed end to fit comfortably into the hand, it can be held against the side and carried securely without hindrance to the running action. Juniors also find it reasonably easy to bounce and catch or continuously bounce a fairly large ball on the run, once they have discovered where to aim in order to avoid interrupting the action of the feet. Similarly, to pat it upwards is quite a simple method of gaining ground with it and may be alternated either with bouncing or with bouncing and catching, although the change of focus involved here complicates matters.

The fact that their attention must also keep changing as they dribble with feet or a stick and try to keep an eye on the positions of other players contributes to children's difficulties with these forms of travelling with a ball; but again, as in bouncing and patting, the major problems here are to keep it at an appropriate distance and to control it with a series of even, rhythmical taps. Even if they do not send it so far ahead as to lose possession of it altogether, or keep it so close as almost to trip over it, they are apt to make a succession of somewhat sporadic prods at the ball and to pursue a rather erratic course punctuated by hesitations and sudden spurts. In particular they often find the management of a hockey or shinty stick troublesome in these circumstances, tending to hold it with hands too far apart and, because the left hand is used ineffectively, sloping it so that the end is brought too close in towards the body and freedom of movement becomes hampered. Most of their difficulties, however, as in all kinds of propelling, may be traced to the relative positions of the feet and ball, and when they scrape it along from behind or it becomes all but lodged between their feet so that the stick is carried immediately in front of the body instead of to the side, it is usually because they are unskilled in adjusting their weight nimbly and quickly.

The transitions from gaining possession of the ball to taking it along, and again from travelling with it to sending it away, are also largely a matter of footwork and general bodily agility, though when the sequence is one of catching, carrying and throwing a large ball, children experience little difficulty once they are able to receive it competently (except when there is any restriction on the number of steps which may be taken during the process).

It is likely that a far richer variety of games than those usually assumed to be suitable for Juniors would evolve if they were challenged to exploit the many possibilities of travelling with a ball and the combinations of these, in conjunction with various methods of receiving it and sending it away. A range of skill in this last type of activity is therefore again desirable for both girls and boys, but in order to achieve any degree of mastery and satisfaction they need to gain such experience in situations in which all three kinds of basic activity are involved. They also need to practise individually as and when appropriate, since it is particularly in this connection that the need for specific techniques which promote economy and efficiency will soon be encountered.

1. Varieties of "travelling with" a ball

(a) Carrying. Opportunities for discovering effective methods of holding and carrying both round and oval balls should be provided, as well as for cradling with a lacrosse stick. Experimenting with a limited number of steps during throwing and catching from one's own throw might also be undertaken.

(b) Propelling along. This includes bouncing and catching; continuous bouncing; patting upwards and alternations of this with bouncing (all of which may similarly be explored in

relation to a particular number of steps with each renewed contact); dribbling with feet; dribbling with a hockey or shinty stick.

2. Apparatus[29]

(a) Objects. It is important that balls should be of the size and weight appropriate to the children, to the particular method of carrying or propelling being adopted and, in both kinds of dribbling, to the condition of the ground (a larger, lighter ball than that normally used aiding less skilled players in keeping it moving).

(b) Implements. It cannot be too strongly urged that Primary children may find considerable difficulty in using hockey, shinty and lacrosse sticks if these are not of the appropriate size, weight, length and proportions.

(c) Obstacles. A selection of posts, skittles, stumps, etc. is useful when children reach the stage of practising dodging but are not able to cope with an opponent on the move.

3. Practice situations

Exploration, experiment and practice in various kinds of carrying and propelling balls along may be:

(a) Individual, aiming to maintain speed over a certain distance, to slow down, to accelerate and to vary speed and change course; to manoeuvre the ball around obstacles and through spaces; and to combine any of these with shooting at a target.

(b) In relation to another who sends the ball conveniently to the receiver, so that after gaining possession of it he runs along,

carrying it with one hand or two;

cradling it in a lacrosse stick;

bouncing it, or alternately bouncing and catching it (each hand might be used in turn or particular attention given to one);

patting it upwards, or alternately patting and bouncing;

dribbling it with feet (attention might be given to both feet equally or particularly to one);

dribbling it with a hockey or shinty stick.

In each of the above cases,

the ball may be sent into the direction into which he will
take it or from the opposite direction so that he has to
change its course completely;

his run may terminate with a shot at a target, or a pass to
another player followed by a repetition of the sequence
of gaining possession, travelling and sending away;

he may attempt to dodge an opponent while in possession
of the ball;

he may attempt to pass the ball before he is tackled but
after he has carried or propelled it at least a little way.

Though the need for agile footwork, speed and good bodily
control in general is probably most apparent when travelling
with a ball occurs, these requirements are, of course, of considerable importance in all games activities, and children
should be helped to become aware of and meet them. While
bodily mastery is to a great extent dependent on overall physical development, certain aspects which have particular relevance in games are often best dealt with in that situation. Skill
in moving nimbly, confidently and safely has to be developed
in relation to striking and throwing, catching and collecting,
and carrying and propelling, as well as in trying to avoid
collisions and to become increasingly aware of positioning.

In general the need to be able to start and stop quickly, to
make a sudden dash as well as to maintain speed over a distance, to run and jump, to swerve, dodge, turn, change direction
and so on is best appreciated within a specific context; similarly, experience in examining what makes for proficiency in
such things and trying to achieve this is best gained in conjunction with other players and with the appropriate apparatus.
But from time to time it may be helpful for children to
experiment and practise without either, and also in a fairly
large rather than a confined space.

Sometimes activities of this nature might be taken with the
class as a whole at the beginning of a lesson, when they serve
the additional purpose in cold weather of getting the children
warm; but their application to the circumstances in which
they have especial importance should always ultimately be
clear to the children so that they participate with understanding and purposefulness.

Various ways in which a lesson may develop, however, belong to the next chapter, which also deals with other practical

considerations arising from the immediate situation of taking a games session.

Note on games apparatus

Manufacturers of sports equipment today produce a useful range of games apparatus which varies in size and weight and is suitable for Primary children.

In addition to sponge and inflated rubber playballs, there are airflow balls from as small as a golf-ball to as large as a Junior netball, and plastic varieties of rounders, football and rugby balls, the last two in sizes 3 and 4 as well as 5. These are considerably cheaper than other kinds and have the advantage of being washable.

Small-sized hockey sticks and cricket bats have been obtainable for some time, and a number of firms are also willing to supply small sizes of tennis rackets and lacrosse sticks. Further variety in bats and sticks is provided by the kinds used in padder tennis, table tennis, rounders, stoolball, softball and shinty. It is important, as previously mentioned, that the size of the handles is not too large for children's hands.

Skittles are available both in wood (either of a pyramid or bottle shape) and in polythene-coated wirework; the latter are not only stable and allow for adjustment at various heights, but are also easily stackable and can be used as hurdles.

Combined rounders/junior jumping stands are a useful dual-purpose item, and another kind of target may be improvised by a hoop lashed to posts. Cradles and folding slip-catchers which have already been referred to in this chapter are available in modern lightweight material and are easily stored; equipment too such as "Jokari" and "Kum Bak" is of direct value for games experience.

Notes

24. *See* footnote 23.

25. This is well illustrated by a boy of ten who, questioned about the appropriateness of repeatedly skying shots which were easy to catch, showed no lack of recognition that these were indeed "gifts" to the opposing fielders, but remarked, "But it's dead good to hit it high!"

26. *See* reference to throwing on page 40.

27. *See* "Note on games apparatus" above.

28. *See* "Note on games apparatus" above.

29. *See* "Note on games apparatus" above.

CHAPTER 8

Organisation and Procedure

The approach to the teaching of games advocated in this book demands of the teacher that he structures situations in which, according to the children's stage of development and preferences in respect of games, they may:

(a) experiment with various ways of using apparatus and devise individual activities based on a selection of these methods;

(b) invent "games" or games-like activities in conjunction with others;

(c) play games (as defined in the narrower sense) of their own invention and also variations of those already known, and solve problems in connection with them.

In this chapter suggestions related to these situations are put forward and their possible place within a lesson, together with the function of the teacher, discussed. First, however, a few general considerations arise which should be taken into account in the early stages of planning a lesson.

Organisation of groups

It will be evident from what has gone before that it is regarded in the main as undesirable for the teacher always to organise a whole class along lines which make for each child doing the same as everyone else in a games lesson. There may, of course, be times when all are drawn together briefly to participate in activities which are of direct relevance to games play in general (as in the case of bodily management, mentioned at the end of Chapter 7), but in the main one would expect as great a variety of individual and group projects to be in progress in the playground or on the games field of a Primary school as often obtains in its classrooms or hall. Obvious reasons for this are the diversity of children's interests and attitudes and the wide range of ability which is bound to exist in any situation of the complexity described in Chapter 2.

Children's ideas and attitudes in respect of games vary enormously according both to individual temperament and to the influence of school, locality and home background. No one can be more easily "conditioned" or is more conservative in certain circumstances than a child. This is clearly evident when, for example, he or she goes to a new school; what goes on there, what the teacher says and does, become, for a time at least, the yardstick for everything else. Thus if the girls play only rounders and the boys cricket, they often accept this state of affairs unquestioningly, in spite of what they do or see happening out of school. Discussions with children usually reveal a considerable gap between what they count as a school game and what they refer to as a game played elsewhere, even when the latter is narrowed down to the kind involving balls and other moving objects. If, however, they are not brought up to think in limited terms of what constitutes the school variety and are encouraged to use their inventiveness in this sphere, they will be found to be refreshingly unprejudiced and ingenious. Also as they move up the Junior school they are often keen to engage in games-like activities, or adaptations of those games, which their parents, brothers and sisters or friends may play, as well as those they see on television; thus they welcome the chance to use rugby balls, baseball sticks, shuttles, various kinds of rackets and so on, even apart from the intrinsic appeal of variety and possible novelty.

1. Ability

The question of grouping according to ability is no more easily settled for the purposes of playing games than in other

fields of activity, the mixing of those of unequal attainment
having both advantages and disadvantages over keeping those
who are more gifted separate from the less able, though not
necessarily less interested, children. It is generally agreed that
one rises to a better level of physically skilled and tactical
performance when participating in a game with good-class
players, whether opponents or members of one's own side,
than in one in which the overall standard is uniformly medi-
ocre. The poorer players stand to gain from the inspiration
and assistance of the better ones who, in turn, are called
upon to be sympathetic and helpful by, for example, "pro-
tecting" their weaker team-mates, making it easy for them to
receive and place passes and so on. On the other hand, it can
be frustrating and restricting for highly competent performers
to be obliged constantly to play with weak ones and not to
be stretched to their limit, just as it may be discouraging
and even depressing for the latter to be matched with those
of a much higher standard.

Other criteria than those applying to physical skill, however,
should surely be considered in any attempt to determine
ability and the ways in which groups might be organised. If
emphasis is placed on the *making* and not merely the playing
of games, it must be recognised that some children, though
not very skilled performers, may be more imaginative and in-
ventive than others with greater technical ability, who might
be less able in terms of originality and powers of adapting
and improvising. Some are also often better observers than
the "natural" player and may be found to excel in experimental and problem-solving situations in which those who
just do the right thing may find it less easy to analyse why.
The mixing of all kinds of players may therefore have good
effects all round, the sharing of ideas and understanding
counting for as much as physical prowess.

2. Sex
The usual practice of automatically segregating the sexes at
the top of the Junior school, and sometimes before, requires
examination. Presumably this is based on the assumption that
boys and girls should, or will in the future, play different

games, but these arguments are difficult to justify educationally except perhaps in the case of some "contact" games.
Differences in physique between girls and boys of Primary
age are hardly such as to prove the determining factors in the
matter of particular games activities requiring certain standards of strength and stamina. It would seem to be as much a
question of temperament as to whether, for example, children
enjoy the rough and tumble of the rugby type of game, and
there may be as many girls at the Primary stage who do as
boys who do not.

Given opportunities to play games of the kind usually
reserved, in many schools at least, for the opposite sex, and
to explore and master techniques in connection with them,
Primary children may be found to profit as much from these
as from games which are generally regarded as peculiarly their
own. This is not to say that girls and boys will not prefer, or
find it beneficial, to separate from time to time, as is also
sometimes likely to happen within certain other school activities; but for it to be an expected and rigid state of affairs
should be challenged. Where mixed classes are taken for
granted as in other lessons, both sexes participate in games in
much the same way as in anything else and gain from an interchange of ideas and preferences. In fact the further one pursues an investigation into which games girls and boys should
be allowed to play in the school situation, the more difficult
it becomes to find good reasons for what tends to obtain at
present, and the more obvious it is that prejudice and erroneous
assumptions hold sway where a more liberal, open-minded
approach is desirable.

As far as the invention of games is concerned there may
well be certain significant considerations to bear in mind. In
our present society it seems that boys are, on the whole,
more knowledgeable about and more influenced by the
national games than are girls. This might sometimes be an advantage, but it can also account for their finding difficulty in
deviating from known forms when comparable apparatus is
used and, as Piaget has tentatively suggested, they seem to
reach the stage of regarding rules as alterable somewhat later
than do girls. On the other hand there is some reason to think

that girls have less interest generally in the elaborate codification of rules than have boys, and outgrow sooner the desire to pursue activities of this kind. There is obviously an interesting field of inquiry here which merits attention. For immediate purposes it seems important to extend similar opportunities to both sexes, and that whatever their standard of play or ultimate preferences in games Primary children should be given experience of a rich variety, of acquiring a wide range of skill and of discovering what there is in common between, as well as what is distinctive about, for example, kicking a football, driving a hockey ball and throwing a netball.

3. Size of group

Certainly what seems to matter to the children themselves more than questions of ability or the mixing of the sexes is the degree of activity permitted by the organisation of numbers (except, of course, insofar as this is affected by factors previously discussed). It is still unfortunately true that owing to the kind of grouping typical of Junior games lessons many children become impatient and restless, and one of the main reasons for this, and for boredom too, is the fact that individuals are not adequately occupied because groups are too large. It is not unusual to see, for instance, a dozen players or more converging on a single ball, or a string of action-starved youngsters waiting long periods for one precious turn to hit (or miss). Yet what they long for most of all is plenty of "goes", whether at striking, throwing, fielding or running with the ball, and small numbers are therefore essential both in order to satisfy their desire for activity and to provide opportunities for the exercise and development of skill in the context of games-like situations.

As we have seen, even two-a-side makes for complexities, especially in the "running" games, and in the "net" and "batting" variety also four can afford considerable challenge and extension of experience. As skill increases, of course, the chance to play with greater numbers and in larger spaces is necessary, but, in the main, groups of not more than ten or twelve in all are usually desirable in order for each child to feel himself (and actually be) an essential part of the proceedings. It is important to note that, left to themselves in this respect, children almost always sort themselves out into groups of the size and composition which they can best manage and which are appropriate for the type of activity selected.

Small numbers also allow for frequent changes of role, a consideration of some importance with young children who enjoy variety and versatility. It is a pity for them to specialise early in certain activities, such as bowling, or in a particular position, such as that of goalkeeper, to the exclusion of others, since they are thus not only restricted in their scope and incompletely challenged but also denied sufficient insight into the nature of the game as a whole. In games of the "batting" kind, therefore, bowler or pitcher, backstop or wicketkeeper, and the various fielders should interchange with one another as well as with the strikers, and in the "running" sort attacking players with defenders.

A final consideration to bear in mind in connection with the organisation of groups is the frequency with which these change. Usually children need to play with the same teammates for a considerable length of time in order to become familiar with them both from the point of view of their technical ability and the contribution they make to the invention of games and the solving of problems. They also need, however, to be able to adapt to others and become used to dealing with unpredictable situations.

Playing areas

Small groups engaged in diverse activities imply a number and variety of playing areas, and the planning of these requires some thought. Ideally they should be of differing sizes in order to cater for and promote different types of games, and it is essential that they are suited to the children's ability both in terms of their skill in using small and large spaces, and also so that points or goals may be scored at not too infrequent intervals.

Markings such as lines and circles on walls or the ground

can be utilised, and defined areas such as netball courts and football pitches can be used crosswise, the normal divisions becoming the sidelines for smaller territories so that greater numbers of children can be accommodated. Since play on grass, even of the same kind of game, is somewhat different from that on a hard surface, it is desirable that both types be provided wherever possible.

Experiments and problems

The structuring of situations for experiment and problem-solving and the place which these may have within a lesson will depend on the children's previous experience, present needs and standards, and should be of direct relevance to the games and games activities in which they engage. Such situations should stimulate curiosity about the behaviour of balls of different kinds, quoits and shuttles, and the ways in which this is determined, and should sharpen their powers of observation, concentration and the desire to improve their skill. A sense of fun and satisfaction in discovery should result both from their explorations and from sharing and utilising their newly-gained knowledge and techniques, and the children themselves should be encouraged to notice what is worth investigating and practising and to put forward suggestions and questions accordingly.

A most important function of the teacher at such times is to set questions and to follow up the children's responses and discoveries. As when making provision for the invention of games, he should ensure that his explanations and inquiries are as simple and brief as possible. Skill in posing questions so as to avoid misunderstanding, and in such a way that the children's attention is directed towards the particular point which he is trying to underline, is as important on the games field as in the classroom; fortunately, children's answers readily show up ambiguous questions (*see* Appendix) and the teacher will probably find by trial and error, if by no other means, how best to use words which, of course, must be suited to their age and background. (Often, if he is somewhat unsuccessful in this respect, the children themselves come to his assistance and translate for one another.)

Both situations and questions should be graded according to the children's ability, and the suggestions given in Chapter 9 are designed to illustrate this. The simplest type of challenge is that related to an activity which can be repeated easily several times and which prompts questions that either imply the relevant answer or offer a simple alternative. For example, in connection with catching a ball dropping from a height:

"Is it best to get directly underneath the ball or to stand a little way away from where it will drop?"

Somewhat more difficult in the same circumstances would be to ask:

"Where do you try to place yourself in relation to the ball?"

For the teacher it may be helpful to make a distinction between what is an "experiment" and what constitutes a "problem". In the former an activity is prescribed and the results observed; in the latter the end is known and it is the means of effecting it which are sought. Thus, in the case of an *experiment,* the children try out a particular way or variety of ways of using apparatus and questions precede or follow this. For example, *prior to* an activity in which an oncoming ball is to be hit *(a)* before, *(b)* after it reaches the body, attention might be directed towards the consequent placing of the ball:

"Find out where the ball goes when you hit it before it reaches you . . . then after . . . ."

Or *following* such an activity:

"What difference did it make to your shot when you struck the ball *(a)* before, *(b)* after it reached your body?"

The same activity could present a *problem* to be solved if the placing of the ball became the major concern, and ways of achieving differing results were tried out and noted. Here again guidance could be given as to what points to observe:

"Notice where the ball is in relation to your body when you hit it . . ."

or the children left to discover this along with other factors influencing the direction of their shot.

A single experiment often, of course, gives rise to several interrelated queries, and a problem may sometimes be solved by more than one method. In the above situation, for instance, the action of the wrists, the angle of the implement at the moment of impact, the transference of weight, the trajectory of the oncoming ball and so on, might well contribute to the outcome, and the interplay of one with another be discovered, or partially discovered.

It will be obvious that discussion between teacher and taught, as well as between the children themselves, will play a more important part in this approach to games than in organising and coaching along conventional lines, but it must be stressed that solutions should be sought by mainly practical means and there should be plenty of scope for action within the process of experiment and discovery. Answers, too, are often better given by demonstration than in words, and this has also the advantage of requiring the whole group, rather than a single individual, to make a positive response to such questions as:

"What shape do your hands make when you catch the ball?" or,
"What do your shoulders do as you throw?"

Dealing with children's responses, both verbal and non-verbal, is a skilled matter, and often requires quick and flexible thinking on the part of the teacher in order to make the best use of their discoveries, and to follow up if need be with further probing. On some occasions it will be appropriate to call the whole class together to pool results, but on others they will be dealt with individually or in groups.

Adequate time must always be allowed for the children to explore the possibilities which spring from a challenge, and some will obviously arrive at conclusions sooner than others. The teacher, moving about among individuals and groups while this is in progress, should note developments and difficulties and give guidance or stimulate further investigation as the need arises. It is important that eventually all the children concerned are helped to arrive at relevant conclusions, whether through their own efforts or through watching others. Comparisons between differing solutions should be made and, in cases where there is a definitely right or wrong answer, the discrepancies should be recognised and reasons for the correct decision made clear. Again, the children themselves may be relied on to explain to one another in a way that is sometimes more effective than those the teacher finds.

For new knowledge to be of value it is, of course, essential that the principle involved is translated into action and that plenty of practice ensues, with the teacher coaching the specific points involved. Opportunities for illustrating its relevance within the context of a games activity should also be exploited as soon and as often as possible.

Invention of games

When children reach the stage of being able and wanting to engage with others in some measure of competitive play and eventually to make a game, the teacher may promote the invention of different kinds by *providing a framework*. This, on the one hand, gives certain limitations and, on the other, delegates a measure of responsibility to the children themselves and allows scope for choice. A parallel exists in the teaching of dance, swimming and gymnastics, and indeed in many other spheres of activity where individuals and groups are helped to make, for example, a dance of their own, a movement sequence, a poem or a play, through the provision of activities and materials which are selected according to their appropriateness and presented as the starting point from which invention may spring.

In a games lesson the teacher might regulate any of the following, leaving the children initially free to decide one or more of the remainder:

1. apparatus;
2. playing areas;
3. rules;
4. number per side.

1. Apparatus

The amount and type of apparatus provided, including targets, goals, etc., obviously determines to a large extent the kind of activities pursued and games invented; it also affects the amount of space required.

2. Playing areas

These again influence considerably the type of activities which evolve. As already pointed out in Chapter 5, "net" games require relatively little space, and if wooden bats with shuttles or airflow balls with sprung bats are used, a group of six or eight children can easily be kept active within a relatively small area. If space is ample the marking of boundaries might be left to the children, who readily adapt them, as in their play out of school, according to their ability and the needs of a game. If, however, space is at a premium the teacher might decide on the apportioning of areas so that, for instance, some groups have sufficient for a "batting" type of game while others are more confined, as in the case of a "net" type of game.

3. Rules

These cover: *(a)* methods of play in terms of the use of implements and/or parts of the body, and the activities involved, and *(b)* scoring.

(a) The kind of games resulting is again largely determined by the nature of the restrictions governing head, hands and feet, and the means of striking, throwing, catching, collecting, carrying and propelling the object.

(b) As previously indicated, Primary children will be found to devise ingenious systems of scoring which are often very different from those of adults but which reflect what they consider the important features of a game. Sometimes, however, they need assistance in adapting methods of scoring so that points are awarded commensurate with the kind of achievement involved as well as with their skill. For example, hitting the net or ring of a netball post might earn a point, although three points or a full goal would remain the result of a netted shot. Sometimes, too (although as a general principle he will encourage attacking play), the teacher might judge it useful for instance to sharpen up the reactions of fielders in a batting game, or to stimulate defence players, by

arranging respectively that catches (which the children themselves frequently take into account in scoring) or the saving
of goals is rewarded.

Rules that the teacher lays down might also be designed to
prevent dangerous play and to ensure that as far as possible
no child becomes a "passenger" or is virtually left out of a
game. In "batting" games, for example, turns might be limited
so that everyone has a chance to bowl and to bat; in "running"
games goals or points might be prohibited until a certain
number of players, or even all, have touched the ball.

4. Number per side

Again, the way children arrange the numbers competing is
often the most suitable for their stage of development and
is an indication of their capacity for social adjustment in the
games situation. Nevertheless, they can be encouraged to vary
the divisions of a group. Six, for instance, can form two teams
of three or consist of three couples who each play against the
other four.

The teacher's selection will depend on such things as the
ability of groups to devise games, on what he sees is popular
at any one time and which may afford the basis for further
development, and on what experience he observes the children
need in order to be able to meet the challenges arising from
the games which evolve.

Having set the scene he does not, of course, then withdraw
completely, shunning responsibility for whatever may happen, or afraid to interfere in the mistaken belief that some
"creative" spark which has at last been kindled will thereby
be extinguished. Teaching along the lines suggested in this
book demands as much, if not more, vigilance and judgment
than are required by traditional methods, and the fact that
the teacher's powers of sensitivity, patience and ingenuity
will be taxed must be squarely faced.

He must, it is true, stand aside to some extent, especially
during the crucial initial stages when the basic features of a
game are being hammered out, and increasingly so as the
children become better able to structure a game and to agree

on necessary modifications as play proceeds. But he must also be ready to intervene and guide when this is required, as well as being alert to the possibilities which emerge that the children could be helped to exploit, either then and there, or on another occasion.

Much will depend, of course, on their training and experience in other spheres of learning and upon the general outlook of the school. Where creative endeavour is encouraged and fostered and the children are used to initiating and carrying out joint projects, the teacher who attempts to adopt similar methods in respect of games activities is likely to have a comparatively easy task. With children who lack such a background, however, he may have to wean them gradually from dependence on him, and there may well be a good deal of discussion and argument both before a game is begun and from time to time while it is in progress. The tidy-minded teacher who likes to see everything going like clock-work may therefore be tempted to step in too soon and take over the organisation himself, and it may at first prove difficult for him not to bring immediate orderliness and smooth-running efficiency into what seems to him a chaotic state of affairs. Yet a certain amount of disorder is often necessary in any situation in which responsibility and a measure of freedom are given to children for the first time.

It should be recognised, however, that this is a stage through which they will pass, and that as familiarity with such situations and training for them increase, the advantages soon begin to be enjoyed and appreciated on both sides (*see* Appendix for children's comments). It is important to remember that any enterprise which is the outcome of corporate effort is always likely to take longer than one determined by a single individual, and that time spent in what at first may appear (and may, indeed, be) something of a muddle is not necessarily wasted.[30] The value, however, lies not only in the end-product achieved, but also in the process by which the problems encountered are analysed and solutions and agreements reached; that is, they are worked out by the participants themselves rather than provided ready-made by an outside agency.

The challenge to the teacher is to decide if and when to intervene and to put his finger on the weak points which are holding up progress. If the children are left to flounder in a morass of difficulty and indecision there may come a point when they grow too frustrated and discouraged to carry on with the project, and if this happens habitually they may develop an antipathy to having to think for themselves in the games situation. Sometimes, however, the teacher may see that a solution is almost within reach, and that given a few more minutes to wrestle with the problems involved the children may achieve success without his assistance, or possibly with only a hint or suggestion. They are indeed often very prepared to compromise in the interests of getting on with a game, as is well illustrated by a case in which a group agreed to play according to one set of rules for half the time and with another for the remainder!

In some instances their ideas may at first be too complex, and they will need the teacher to help them to clarify such things as rules and scoring in order to progress towards simplicity. In other cases an invented game may prove insufficiently challenging for their abilities, and adaptations in order to increase its difficulty may be required; upper Juniors readily appreciate that an easy game is often not an interesting one. A certain balance has to be maintained between encouraging children to modify their games as the need arises and to adhere to what has been evolved by common consent. The less experienced they are, the more apt they will be to substitute one idea for another, so that the original invention becomes rapidly unrecognisable; but again, this is a stage that may quickly pass.

As previously mentioned, games similar to those of the major kind will probably arise from time to time, especially at the top of the Junior school, differing in such things as types of side, boundaries and scoring. When this happens the teacher might consider whether this is an appropriate moment to introduce some of the rules of the full game through eliciting such knowledge as the children might already have, through helping them to use rule books, through direct explanation or through a combination of these methods.

Procedure

The amount of time devoted in any one session to experimental activity and/or to the invention of a game will, of course, vary according to the stage of development and preferences of the children, but in most cases probably one or two investigations only will be found to be sufficient.

For some groups the plan might be as follows:

(a) the lesson begins with a game, whether already known or newly invented;

(b) the game is suspended as problems arise and/or weaknesses become evident;

(c) one or two of these problems are selected for investigation, the children as well as the teacher playing a part in deciding which aspects of the game require attention and, if appropriate, various members of the group carrying out different experiments;

(d) discoveries are shared and solutions examined;

(e) the techniques involved are practised and coached;

(f) the game is resumed with particular concentration on the points to which attention has been drawn.

If time permits, further experiments developing from the original might ensue after (d).

Alternatively, a particular aspect of play which has proved in previous sessions to be weak or neglected might be taken as the starting point. This might be decided in the classroom before the lesson begins and here again the children should be encouraged to put forward their own suggestions. For example, it might be recalled that in a game of the "running" type in which a netball was used and throwing was one of the main activities the passes were all of one kind, namely, from one player's hands to another's. The procedure might then be:

(a) the problem is set for pairs or small groups within the main group to find other appropriate ways of passing;

(b) the various findings are compared;

(c) a particular pass, for instance, the bounce-pass, is selected and points in connection with its usefulness noted;

(*d*) the original game is resumed with the stress on varieties of passing, including of course the new one just discovered, and the children helped to recognise the circumstances when each is specially applicable. This affords an instance of when the teacher might lay down a particular rule in relation to scoring, such as that the final pass had to be a bounce-pass in order to score a goal or point, or he might leave it to the children to work out how the incorporating of this new technique be rewarded.

Sometimes a group could begin with experiments and/or problems in connection with a particular activity or technique which then becomes of major importance in a game, points being scored in direct relation to it. In other words a "theme" is first explored and then used as a basis for invention. This "theme" might be an activity which the teacher has noticed is in vogue, say, during lunch-breaks, and which offers scope for further variation and development. If, for example, he sees that keeping a ball aloft is popular, he could set problems related to this designed to increase skill and versatility, and then present a framework for a game in which keeping the ball in the air becomes the main feature of play and of scoring. Needless to say, there will be no shortage of ideas coming from the children as to what is in fashion at any one time.

Finally, there is no need for every session to include either experiments or new inventions. When a group has evolved a game which is satisfying and can be remembered it is a pity not to give the children opportunities simply to play it and to become more skilful as they do so. Particularly when periods are short a whole lesson might from time to time be devoted to games that are already familiar. Children also often enjoy teaching one another games they have invented, and both types of game require that they clarify the details and provide a realistic situation in which verbal instruction is necessary.

To sum up, then, there are at least four possible orders of procedure.

(*a*) Game; experiments and problems arising from that game; resumed game.

    (b) Experiments and problems in connection with particular activities requiring improvement; game (*either* in which the relevant discoveries are incorporated incidentally, *or* in which they are directly linked with methods of play and scoring).

    (c) Experiments related to an activity or activities known to be popular; game based on this.

    (d) Game or games.

For the teacher who does not at first feel prepared to alter wholesale his methods of dealing with a games session, but who yet recognises the need to try to bring about a measure of reform in his teaching in this sphere, it might be worth mentioning that something in the nature of a compromise may be found which later enables him to give further trials to the methods advocated in this book. He might, perhaps, while retaining the practice of presenting children (one hopes, on a voluntary basis) with ready-made games, endeavour to link these with experiments and problems as in *(a)* and *(b)* above. Alternatively he might adhere to traditional practices and training in specific techniques but attempt to structure situations in which the children use these in games of their own invention.

The class teacher who deals with a variety of subjects will also find that plenty of opportunities exist outside the games period itself (and not merely on wet days) for deepening and extending children's interest and understanding in this sphere, and for drawing upon it to advantage in association with other activities. Children often enjoy talking about games, as is probably evident to teachers of Juniors whenever they give them a free choice of topic for a lecturette or written essay; and to describe and explain experiments, inventions, and such things as possible modifications to a game can provide a good starting point for discussion and writing. It can also be of advantage to them to reflect on certain aspects of play out of the context of the actual practical situation, as well as serving to help the teacher to check what has been understood in terms of rules, methods of scoring and the like.

Juniors often prove to be excellent instructors and coaches

themselves, and take delight, both on and off the field, in teaching one another the games they have devised and giving advice on how to improve and umpire. A class repertoire of original games may thus be built up as with favourite songs, poems, dances and so on, with special names given to distinguish them and perhaps books compiled as a record. Children of nine and ten years of age who were asked to write about their experiences in making up their own games (*see* Appendix) showed considerable concern for detail and exactness, and often included diagrams and drawings of such things as pitches, positions of players and targets, and even the equipment. Frequent reference to the length, size, weight and proportions of balls, implements and other apparatus, in addition to playing areas, indicated several possibilities of linking such observations with mathematics and physics, while interest among Juniors is usually easily aroused in the origins of games, what people played in other ages and what is popular in other parts of the world today.

As with any subject that captures their interest and imagination, Primary children are most resourceful and enterprising in conducting "research" both in and out of school into games and allied topics such as the kind of clothing worn at a particular time or the behaviour of spectators, and they often undertake "homework" in this connection with enthusiasm. The girl who mentions getting an idea about improving a game several days after the lesson in which it was first played (*see* p. 124) is probably typical of not a few children who continue to think about certain problems that arise and ways of solving them.

Since at this age they also have a marked tendency to classify and order information, there is every reason to suppose that they would find satisfaction in attempting to establish categories of games and to sort out what are common "ingredients" along lines similar to those pursued in the foregoing pages. The classification proposed in this book is by no means regarded as wholly comprehensive or final, and a child's readiness to point out the exception to a general principle might well contribute to a more acccurate analysis and/or synthesis.

Any suggestion that as a result of the time devoted to experimenting, problem-solving and the inventing of games, the standard of play among Primary children will be lower than if they concentrated from the first on a few ready-made games may therefore be resisted. Such a claim implies an assumption that it is by performance alone that the value of games activity in education should be judged, whereas it is the authors' contention that knowledge about and experience of games can, and should, be integrated with the rest of the curriculum: many children who would probably make little contribution to the traditional kind of games lesson and derive meagre benefit from it are likely to gain as players, umpires and spectators from the kind of approach that is here advocated. There are, in any case, no grounds for believing that an introduction to a wide range of skills necessarily leads to poorer achievement in specific techniques—indeed the contrary may well prove to be the case, a broadly-based programme ultimately resulting in higher standards of play as well as of interest and understanding.

Notes

30. It may be possible to use classroom time to deal with some or-ganisational problems, and if also children are expected to come to a games lesson having already discussed and planned their requirements, and are well trained in dealing with equipment, valuable playing time can be saved.

CHAPTER 9

Examples of Experiments and Problems

The suggestions in this final chapter are intended as a guide only and are not in any way a comprehensive coverage of experiments and problems, but they do indicate some of the main kinds of these. Examples are given of types of question which can be adapted for children of a variety of ages and those who are at different stages of development.

Teachers should find it helpful to refer to previous chapters in conjunction with this one. Chapters 4 and 6 contain much of the material on which experiments and problems are based and provide further ideas for questions, as well as supplying information required for the answers. Some experiments and problems are related specifically to each of the three basic types of activity but, as already stated, throwing and striking are seldom isolated from catching and collecting and both are frequently linked with travelling. Consequently in the last section situations are presented in which two, or all three, activities are combined and as such should be considered more advanced.

There is no particular significance in the way in which the questions are worded; all the methods suggested in Chapter 8, which dealt also with the structuring of situations, are employed and of course teachers will often need to make certain modifications to meet the requirements of the particular occasion.

Striking and throwing

Situation 1. Two children a short distance apart and throwing a small ball to each other.

Suggestion. Try to find different ways of sending the ball to your partner

(a) so that it does not touch the ground,
(b) using the ground.

Question. How many ways of sending the ball did you find? Show these.

Response. Variations of *underarm* and *overarm* throws will probably be shown as well as *rolling* the ball along the ground and *bouncing* it.

Situation 2. Two children throwing a small ball to each other and trying to increase the distance between them.

Suggestion. Find the most effective way of sending the ball to each other at a variety of distances.

Question. Did you discover whether the same sort of throw was effective at any distance or that at a particular distance you had to alter the method in some way?

Response. The answers should indicate that the children recognise that at certain distances underarm throwing is more efficient and desirable, but that beyond a particular distance, which will vary with individuals, an overarm throw results in the ball travelling faster and further.

Situation 3. A group of children engaged in a "batting" activity. Bowling is underarm and taking place within a square, but no attempt is being made to use the square to advantage.

Suggestion. Experiment with different methods of underarm delivery and discover what use can be made of preliminary steps. Can you deceive the batsman in any way?

Questions. Keeping within the square but using it to the best advantage what different methods of approach did you find? What use can be made of this knowledge to outwit the batsman?

Responses. Four kinds of approach are shown in the diagrams below. Their uses are that in

(a) more momentum can be gained than from a standing delivery;

(b) because the bowler begins with his back to the batsman, there is an element of surprise;

(c) inswing and

(d) outswing can be produced (assuming a right-handed batsman).

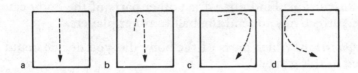

The bowler can also vary the speed of his delivery as well as disguising it: for example, accelerating in the preliminary run but controlling the ball at the last minute and bowling a slow ball.

Situation 4. A "batting" game is in progress in which overarm bowling is being employed. Although the children have acquired a degree of accuracy they lack the subtlety that the teacher judges they are capable of achieving by spinning the ball.

Suggestion. Bowl overarm to a partner and find out what happens when you use your fingers actively as you release the ball.

Questions.

(a) What happened to the ball as it rebounded?

(b) Can you relate the use of the fingers to what happened to the ball on bouncing?

Responses.

(a) The ball can be made to "break" to the right or left.

(b) To make a ball "break" to the right on contact with

the ground it must spin clockwise and therefore (for a right-arm bowler) be released off the index finger. To make it "break" to the left it must spin counter-clockwise and be released out of the back of the hand.

(In this connection some children may well discover the importance of the approach run and also of the body action as a whole, but the mastery of these is usually beyond Juniors.)

Situation 5. A "running" game is being played quite skilfully with hands only being used to control the ball. The teacher decides that this particular group needs a more challenging situation.

Suggestion. Find out which other parts of the body can be used effectively to send the ball to other players.

Question. Which parts of the body did you decide could be used in this game?

Response. Head and feet will be among the answers given.

Further questions.
(a) When you kick a ball which part of the foot do you use?
(b) Where do you focus your attention as you prepare to head the ball?
(c) Which part of the head is it best to use?
(d) How does the rest of the body help in these two actions?

Responses.
(a) The part of the foot used will be determined by the type of shot required; for example, if a ball is to be lofted the toe and the top surface of the foot will be used, whereas if it is to be tapped to one side then that side of the foot will be used.

(Children could also try to discover what is involved in making a ball swerve and the similarities in this respect with what is involved in making the ball "break" as in Situation 4.)

(b) On the ball.
(c) The forehead.

(d) The arms particularly should be used to help to keep the body balanced.

Situation 6. Children are playing individually with lightweight bats and small balls and a few are attempting to make several consecutive hits.

> *Suggestion.* Try to make several hits without the ball touching the ground.

> *Questions.*
> (a) Where do you look?
> (b) How do you make use of your feet?
> (c) Should you try to keep the ball near to the bat?
> (d) Is your arm held stiffly or easily?

> *Responses.*
> (a) The eyes should be fixed on the ball.
> (b) The weight should be on the balls of the feet which should be kept moving with small steps according to where the ball goes.
> (c) Yes (although this does not mean that the ball is not struck actively).
> (d) Easily (a flexible action of elbow and wrist is important).

Situation 7. A group of children playing a "batting" game using a rounders stick and a small ball. The batsmen are consistently making contact but failing to hit to any great distance.

> *Suggestion.* Discover what produces a strong hit.

> *Questions.*
> (a) How should you stand while waiting for the ball to be bowled?
> (b) Where should your attention be directed?
> (c) What do you do as the ball leaves the bowler's hands?
> (d) What do you do as you make contact with the ball and immediately afterwards?
> (e) Describe the pathway the bat makes.

Responses.

(a) With feet apart and sideways on to the bowler. The weight can be equally distributed over both feet, knees slightly flexed, or the weight can be more over the front foot ready to sway back as the stick is swung back in preparation for the hitting action.

(b) The batsman should watch the bowling action, but once the ball is released the eyes must be kept on the ball itself.

(c) The stick should be swung back as the weight is transferred to the back foot.

(d) The stick should be brought through with an easy swing to contact the ball as the weight is transferred forward. If the weight of the body has been behind the hit the swing will need to be completed and a follow-through of the arm and stick will result.

(e) The preparatory swing and the action may be made along the same line, or the two may fuse to describe a curved pathway. Some children may relate the stick to the body and include the fact that the stroke may be completed with the swing bringing the stick across or away from the body.

Further question. Is there anything similar about hitting a ball and throwing it?

Response. The preparatory stance is similar, so too is the weight transference, the shoulder action and the follow-through.

Situation 8. As in 7 but in this instance although the ball is being hit powerfully the children show little ability to vary its direction.

Suggestion. Experiment in small groups to discover what determines the direction of a ball when hit.

Questions. What relation, if any, did you find between the direction into which the ball was sent and

(a) the placing of your feet;

(b) the position of the bat on contact with the ball in relation to the body?

Responses (for the right-handed batsman).

(a) The use of the feet is important in the placing of the ball. If the ball is to be hit to the left of the bowler then the left foot of the batsman should not only be in front of the right but across it—in fact the front foot should indicate the direction into which the batsman wishes to hit the ball. If the ball is to pass the bowler on his right then the batsman stands more squarely on to the bowler.

(b) If the ball is to be hit to the left of the bowler then the ball is taken "late", that is, the batsman waits until the ball has passed the body. (This often results in the weight remaining on the back foot during the hitting action.) If the ball is to be hit to the right of the bowler then it is taken "early", that is, before it reaches the body.

Further questioning could lead the children to explore the possibilities of hitting behind the wicket in certain of the "batting" games, and to discover that strokes can be made off both the front and back foot; drives into the area in front of the wicket often result in a transference of weight forward, those sent square to the wicket and behind it are often hit off the back foot.

Situation 9. A "net" game is in progress with the children using hands only to keep the ball airborne. The rallies are rather short owing to lack of skill.

Suggestion. Try to find a number of ways of using your hands to keep the ball up in the air.

Questions.

(a) What part(s) of the hand(s) can be used?

(b) If the ball is dropping below head height how can you still keep it off the ground?

(c) If it is above head height where should you aim to be in relation to it to make a good return?

(d) Describe the action of the arms in the latter instance.

Responses.

(a) The fingers, palm, fist and "heel" of the hand(s).

(b) The hips must be lowered and the hands used palms uppermost.

(c) Underneath the ball.

(d) The arms should be flexed and fingers ready to push the ball away and direct it either into the air or over the net.

Catching and collecting

Situation 1. A group of children playing a "batting" game in which the fielding is inadequate.

Suggestion. In twos find out which are the best methods of fielding a ball which is—

(i) rolling along the ground towards you,

(ii) bouncing up off the ground,

(iii) dropping from above.

Questions.

(a) Where do you position yourself in each case?

(b) Is it important to watch the ball all the time?

(c) Do you wait for the ball to come to you?

Responses.

Question (a), (i) and (ii). Behind the ball and slightly to the side of it (the side will be determined by whether the player is right- or left-handed). At first it might be necessary to encourage children to get in a direct line with the ball and collect it in two hands, but later they can try approaching to one side (left for right-handed children), so that they collect it with one hand ready immediately for a return throw. (iii) Try to get almost under the ball.

Question (b) Yes. (This is a most important point for children to grasp.)

Question (c) It is better to move to meet the ball so as to reach it as early as possible; this may involve a jump in (iii).

Further questions. If you are fielding near to the batsman

(a) how can you prepare yourself to field the ball quickly?

(b) how can you anticipate where the ball is going to be hit?

(c) If you are a wicket-keeper how can you tell which way the ball will bounce?

Responses.

(a) Adopt a mobile stance, crouching slightly with the weight over the balls of the feet.

(b) By watching the feet of the batsman you can often predict where the ball will go if hit; also by watching where the ball is hit in relation to the batsman's body.

(c) Often by watching the hand and particularly the wrist of the bowler.

Situation 2. A "running" game is in progress involving play with the hands and feet, but the children are not freeing themselves successfully from their opponents.

Suggestion. Find out what ways there are of getting away from a defender who is marking you closely, so that you receive the ball successfully.

Questions.

(a) How can you make use of a change of direction?

(b) How can you make use of a change of speed?

Responses.

(a) You can pretend to go to the right and make a preliminary move, which might be only a step or a sway of the body, into that direction, but make the final move (that is, several steps) into the opposite direction. Or you can pretend to move forward, but after feinting in that direction drop back, and vice versa.

(b) A sudden sprint or an abrupt stop can be used to deceive an opponent.

Further question. When attempting to get free how can you assist the player with the ball to get it to you successfully?

Response. Dodge purposefully, that is, decide where you are going; get free in an appropriate position relative to his position, and make a clear indication as to where the ball is to be passed.

Situation 3. A "running" game is being played involving the use of hockey sticks, and the children are finding difficulty in receiving the ball from different directions.

Suggestion. In twos experiment with collecting the ball on the stick when it is coming

(*a*) from backward left,
(*b*) from backward right,
(*c*) from in front of you.

Questions.
(*i*) Do you move to meet it?
(*ii*) Where is your attention directed?
(*iii*) Where is your stick in relation to your body?
(*iv*) When do you attempt to contact the ball?

Responses.
(*a*) If it is travelling slowly, go to meet the ball without turning your back to the direction in which you are going to run, and keeping to the right of the ball. Look over your left shoulder, keeping the stick on the right side of the body. Allow the ball to cross in front of your feet and on to your stick on the right of the body before you contact it.

(*b*) Look over your right shoulder, twist the body and place your stick slightly behind and to your right, keeping it near the ground; angle the blade so that it faces the ball, "give" on contact and re-direct the ball with a series of taps so that it does not cross to your left but goes ahead.

(*c*) Move to meet the oncoming ball keeping your stick close to the ground and to the right of the body, with the blade squarely facing the ball. The body should be reaching forward slightly but on contact with the ball there should be a "give" in the body, including your arms, which draw the stick towards you. The ball should be kept slightly ahead and to your right.

Carrying and propelling

Situation 1. A "running" game is being played in which travelling while bouncing the ball is a feature. The children, however, have not sufficiently mastered this skill to be able to use it successfully while maintaining the speed of the game.

Suggestion. In twos (one observing the other) bounce a ball keeping more or less on the spot, and then bounce it but keep on the move travelling forwards.

Questions.
(a) How does the direction into which your partner bounces the ball vary in the two cases?
(b) Does he use the palm of the hand or the fingers?
(c) At approximately what height does he bounce the ball when he is on the move at a reasonable speed?

Responses.
(a) In the first instance the ball should be directed straight downward while in the second it is propelled forward at an angle.
(b) Although the whole hand is used it is the fingers which, because of their flexibility, are instrumental in directing and spinning the ball; the wrist action in also most important.
(c) Between knee and waist height.

Further experiments could be set in connection with movement into different directions, zig-zagging and swerving, and dodging a partner. Suggestions could be made which direct attention to the important part the feet play in manoeuvring the ball.

Situation 2. Hockey sticks are being used in a "running" game but the flow is hampered by the children's inability to dribble well.

Suggestion. In twos (one observing the other) find out the best way of keeping the ball close to the stick and maintaining an average running speed.

Questions.
(a) Are the hands together or apart on the stick? Is the right below the left or vice versa?
(b) Where is the stick carried in relation to the body?

(c) Does he hit the ball and run after it or tap it along keeping it close to the stick?

Responses.
(a) The hands are a little way apart with the right hand below the left.
(b) The stick is carried to the right and slightly in front of the body.
(c) He should tap it along keeping it close to the stick.

Further question. Dribble the ball clockwise around another player and describe the relative paths of the ball and your feet.

Response. The ball follows a smaller curve than that made by the feet. (The feet will be in the normal running position but the trunk will be turned to face the ball.)
Similarities could be discussed between dribbling a ball with the feet and with a stick.

The number of questions in this section is limited as problems arise from situations in which travelling is linked with other activities rather than from specific skills themselves.

Collecting and throwing

Situation. A "batting" game is being played in which quick returns to a target are vital but the children are slow to convert collecting into throwing.

Suggestion. Explore the following situations with a partner.

(a) No. 1	Ball	No.2
(b) No. 2	No. 1	Ball

No. 1 in each case runs to pick up the ball and returns it as quickly as possible to No. 2.

Question. What differences did you discover, if any, in the way you returned the ball to No. 2?

Responses. In *(a)* the return is an underarm throw because less bodily adjustment is needed and the distance is such that an underarm throw is the more appropriate.

In *(b)* an overarm throw is used because the thrower in this case has to turn in order to return the ball and it will be found that as he turns the throwing arm is correctly placed for this throw.

The children themselves could be challenged to suggest other practices with a partner which highlight this problem, and a further suggestion might be made.

Further suggestion. No. 1 and No. 2 stand side by side—No.1 rolls the ball gently along the ground and No. 2 runs to pick it up. No. 2 sees how quickly he can overtake the ball and return it.

Further questions.
(a) Do you pick the ball up with one or two hands?
(b) Do you overtake it and turn to pick it up or do you collect it while you are running beside it?
(c) As you collect the ball is your palm or the back of your hand uppermost?

In each case give reasons for your answer.

Responses.
(a) With one hand—preferably the throwing hand. In a game then no time is wasted in making use of the ball, that is, returning it to bowler or base.
(b) Preferably pick it up while running beside it. (This will depend very much on the skill of the individual.) The reason is again less waste of time.
(c) The ball should be collected with the back of your hand uppermost, so that it is ready for the return throw.

Throwing and collecting

Situation. A group of children playing a "running" game which involves the ball being bounced or thrown to one another, and players are not allowed to travel once they are in possession of the ball. The passing is not sufficiently skilful to allow a fluent game to proceed, and play has become rather static.

Suggestion. In twos find out where the ball has to be placed if a running player is to receive it in such a way that he can throw it almost immediately.

Questions.
(*a*) Do you aim the ball at your partner? If not where should you send it? Why?
(*b*) What do you have to take into account in judging where it should go?
(*c*) If he is marked to which side of him should you try to get it?
(*d*) If you are bouncing the ball to your partner how can you make it easy for him to receive it?

Responses.
(*a*) The ball should be sent into *a space* where you judge the receiver will be when he catches it, and to the right for a right-handed player if possible, so that the follow-through of the receiving action can merge into the main action.
(*b*) The speed, direction and ability of the receiver.
(*c*) To the free side of the player receiving it.
(*d*) The bounce should make contact with the ground so that it is rising to about shoulder height as it is caught and should not be directed at the feet of the receiver.

Travelling and sending away

Situation. A "running" game with a hockey stick is being played, and it is noticed that the majority are not able to change readily from dribbling the ball to hitting it to other players.

Suggestion. Find out what changes should occur at the point when dribbling must be converted into driving.

Questions.
(*a*) Does the grip on the stick alter? If so, how?
(*b*) Do you have to adjust your feet in any way if you want to send the ball
  (*i*) to the left,
  (*ii*) to the right?

Responses.

Question *(a)* The hands should be drawn nearer together at the top of the stick in order to drive.

Question *(b)(i)* No, because the stick is merely swung across the body as the ball is struck. *(ii)* In order to send a ball to the right you should quickly adjust your feet so that they face the direction into which the ball is to be hit, that is, your right. The quickest method involves a pivot on the right and a step onto the left as the stroke is made.

Collecting and travelling

Situation. A "running" game is being played which involves the use of lacrosse sticks—the fluency and progress of the game are impeded owing to the children's lack of skill in picking up the ball once it is grounded and converting this into travelling with it.

Suggestion. Find the best ways of collecting a ball from the ground
  (i) when it is stationary;
  (ii) when it is travelling away from you;
  (iii) when it is travelling towards you.

Questions.
  (a) Where is the crosse carried while you are approaching the ball?
  (b) Is the ball collected while you are on the move or should you stop to pick it up?
  (c) What happens bodily during the collecting action?
  (d) What word do you think best describes the whole action?
  (e) What should you do immediately the ball is in your possession if you wish to travel with it?

Responses.

Question *(a)* In each instance the crosse should be carried as for the normal running action, that is, across your body with hands apart ready for cradling.

Question *(b)* In *(i)* and *(ii)* you should run onto the ball preparing for the collecting action when approximately

2—3 yards from the ball. In *(iii)* there will probably be a slight hesitation while you collect the ball, as this involves a sudden drop onto the ball.

Question *(c)* You lower your hips, keeping your head over the ball and with your leading foot reaching towards it.

Question *(d)* A "scoop".

Question *(e)* As soon as the ball is collected you should assume the cradling position of the crosse and begin the cradling action as quickly as possible.

Throwing, collecting and travelling

Situation. A "running" game with a football has been evolved in which throwing and kicking are allowed and players may travel with the ball either dribbling or carrying it along, but may only pass it backwards. The children are finding difficulty in *(a)* collecting the ball from ground level with the hands and *(b)* sending a backward pass, and the game is constantly being interrupted.

Suggestions.
(a) In twos find the best way of running onto a ball and picking it up without losing speed.
(b) In threes find out what is involved in achieving a successful running, backward pass.

Questions.
(a) *(i)* Do you lower your body in the approach run gradually or do you wait until you are almost within reach of the ball before you drop onto it? Where should you be in relation to the ball when you collect it from the ground?
(ii) What is a difficulty you find that would not occur when picking up a small ball?
(b) If you are carrying the ball in two hands, what happens to the upper half of the body when you have to throw to backward right or backward left?

Responses.
(a) *(i)* You should "swoop" onto the ball, at the last possible moment dropping the hips in order to do so.

You should be above it and to one side, that is, not directly behind it.

(ii) Both hands have to be used and this necessitates a twist of the trunk as you drop onto the ball to collect it.

(b) Your trunk twists to the right or left as your hands and arms prepare to release the ball into that direction.

Wherever appropriate, reference should be made to the children's past experience so that similarities are established and they are helped to apply their knowledge of one situation to another of a like nature. This may occur more readily and frequently once the children become aware of certain basic features which underlie games skills; nevertheless the teacher should seize any opportunity which presents itself to draw their attention to the common factors which underlie all games and which are noted in detail in Chapters 4 and 6.

APPENDIX

Children's Comments

An insight into children's responses to the methods of teaching recommended in this book is provided by:

    (a) extracts from written work of nine- and ten-year olds who were asked to comment on a series of lessons in which they had been given opportunities to invent their own games, formulate rules and conduct experiments in relation to these, including any alterations which they considered might improve these games in any way, and

    (b) samples from answers given during the lessons themselves.

Elaboration or explanation is superfluous as there seems no doubt as to where the children's priorities lie and what, for them, is the "essence" of a game. (An asterisk indicates that the sex of the child is not known to the authors.)

Comments on original inventions
and the playing of these games

Nine-year-olds

"Of all the games I enjoyed the most and that is quite a few I enjoyed those which we devised ourselves." (Boy)

"I liked playing our game best because you could make up

your own rules and also because everyone can be doing something." (Boy)

"I liked it best because it was always going and it was exciting." (Boy)

"I liked it best because you used more of your body . . . and because its lively and exciting." (Boy)

"I liked our games because you are all ways doing something." (*)

"I liked it best because there was a lot of running in it and this is something I enjoy." (Girl)

"The game I liked best is stoolball because there is not to much running in it." (Girl)

"I like to play cricket because you don't get so tired has much as the other games, and I like bowling and batting."(Boy)

"The game I liked best was the one our group made up. It was a kind of mixture between, say, rugby and tag. I liked it because it had plenty of action in it and it was fast, but it was better than football because you could always use your hands if you so wished." (Boy)

"I very much enjoyed playing it nobody is left standing and doing nothing." (Girl)

"I liked it because everybody has a chance of either kicking, hitting or throwing the ball." (Boy)

Ten-year-olds

"The game I liked best was one with a big net across like a tennis net. I liked it best because it was unusual and fun to play and it wasn't a game of arguements, you usually start a argument when someone is out and thinks they shouldn't be." (Girl)

"I liked this game best because nobody was just standing or sitting around with nothing to do at all." (*)

"The game I liked best hasn't got a name but it is a bit like cricket in all ways. I liked it best because everybody is doing something all the time." (Boy)

"The game I liked best I think was our own version of rounders. I liked this best because we made the game so every one was doing something and not standing around, even if you where out you could field or keep the score." (Girl)

Comments on own rules

Nine-year-olds

"We made these rules because the game wouldn't be much fun otherwise." (Girl)

"We made certain rules which have prevented quarrells." (Boy)

"We then had a five minute discussion about rules and the scoring system. This is what we came up with. . . ." (Boy)

"The following rules were selected because they seemed to run smoothly. . . ." (Boy)

". . . so that at least everyone got two innings you were out when you had made ten runs." (Boy)

". . . these rules are so that ever one gets a turn at batting." (Girl)

". . . this is so that the ball moves round every person." (Girl)

". . . and the centre pass is taken by one of the losing side." (Boy)

". . . the rules were that you could not get more than ten runs for your team in one innings, but if you had nine runs and hit a six you would be out for fifteen." (Boy)

"I suggested you should get two points for stumping bowler's position, and three for a catch." (Girl)

"The team of 9 had to split into three groups of three named A, B, and C. 'A' team was in first and B and C team had to field." (Girl)

"On the fielding side they could score two points for a catch and one for stumping a player out." (Girl)

"If you are not batting you have to field so you are always moving about. For a catch one person is out and the person who catches it gets a point for his team if he is really on the fielding side, if he is not really on the fielding side the person is not out and he does not get a point." (Girl)

"If somebody is out off the bating side then they have to help the fielders to field." (Girl)

"There is no going right up to the net and throwing the ball down." (Girl)

"If you are right-handed you are not allowed to hit as if left-handed." (Girl)

"The rules we use are there is one person batting at each post and if one person is out the other person has to try and get points by himself, when both people are out two others come in. *There are no sides.*" (Boy)

"We found we needed four posts for the running and one as a bating post." (Boy)

Ten-year-olds

"We had our rules different from the proper ones, we had for instance every time you hit the ball you had to run and very fast bowls were not allowed and a very long distance hit was a four." (Boy)

"You scored by touching the ball down between the two posts and then there was a convertion where you had to kick the ball through the two posts but this time you had to kick the ball past a goal keeper but even if you missed you got two points for a try." (Boy)

". . . this is because their would be a lot of foul play. . . . because if they did the game would turn very ruff." (Girl)

"The rules we made were quite a few. First of all a person got two pieces of straw one short the other long . . . then the two captains picked a hand and the one which had the longest straw their team started." (Girl)

". . . then the game would be stopped for a few precious minutes, But we always sorted it out in the end and the game would continue." (Boy)

Suggested improvements to existing rules

"If the net was higher it would be harder to score. I also think that if the ball was heavier it would be more difficult. Also if there were less a side you would have more to do." (Girl)

"I think a good improvement is that the bowler has to hit the white square three times until the person is out so he and his team get more points and the batter gets more points." (Girl)

"I think that the teams should be mixed of boys and girls and not a lot of friends together." (Boy)

"Also it should be not only for girls but for boys as well."
(Boy)

"Everybody on the fielding side to change over every so
often e.g. fielder becoming back stump, back stump becoming
baller, baller becoming fielder." (Girl)

". . . and they bat from youngest to oldest." (Boy)

"No fancy catching." (Girl)

"Now I thought the fielding sides should score, so for a
catch 2 points." (Girl)

"We suggested a boundry line which was the teams court
so you could score more runs." (Boy)

"I didn't really approve of many . . . one was simply crazy
. . . another I thought of half way through Monday the 26th
June was . . . ." (Girl)

"And most important if you loose be good sports." (Girl)

*Examples of the practicality of children and their desire to
cover all eventualities*

"You need two balls (if one gets lost.)" (Girl)

"You need paper and pencil to keep the score." (Girl)

". . . some means of identifying the two teams." (*)

Some titles given by children to invented games

"Round-Crick", "Kick and Throw", "Triangles", "Boardball", "Bodyball", "Fistyball".

"My favourite game is boardball. It might have been thought
of before but I haven't hear of it so I have bestowed upon it
the 'Boardball'. It is derived from netball." (*)

In their writings only two children mentioned results: one
referred to her side winning, another girl mentioned the number of points scored and named the members of the team.

*Examples of children's answers to questions asked during
games lessons*

Q. "How do you stand when batting?"
A. "Sideways with weight on the back foot."
Q. "When fielding from a distance is it better to throw the
ball or run with it to the bowler?"

A. "Throw it overarm."

Q. "How do you stand when beginning this throw?"

A. "Sideways, weight on the back foot bending low to to the ground."

Q. "What do you have to do to throw a ball a long way?"

A. "You need three fingers curled round the ball with the index finger and the thumb straight."

Q. "How can you hit the ball with more force?"

A. "Hold the bat with two hands."

Q. "Do you think it is a good idea to try and hit the ball high into the air or fairly low?"

A. "Somebody might catch it if you hit it high, but it's dead good hitting it high."

Q. "Do you keep your hands and arms extended after catching the ball?"

A. "No, they are brought towards the body and then to one side."

Q. "Why to one side?"

A. "Because the body is in the way."

Answers obviously indicating the need for either further questions or the re-framing of the original question

Q. "How do you hold the bat when batting?"

A. "To one side with the flat surface facing forwards."

Q. "Why have you chosen to bowl underarm in this game?"

A. "Because it gets to the person."

Q. "How do you stand to hit a ball?"

A. "Facing it."

Q. "How do you grip your bat?"

A. "Like a spoon."

Q. "Why are you using your feet in this game?"

A. "Because we are playing football."

The reader's attention is drawn to the following two comments in which the children's awareness of the pleasure derived is not only from the action itself, as in the previous examples, but from the sensations of the action.

"I love hitting the ball and hearing the click off the bat and I like bowling and catching it and throwing it long distances and watching the wicket being knocked out of place." (Boy)

"The game I like best is rounders the reason for this I think is the way you start with teeth about to chatter on a cool day or just a refreshing tempritour on a warm day, then a little later you are nearly clappsing with heat and exhortion and also the feal of the wind as you run against it you are sweating but cool all at the same time which sends a sensation through your body." (Girl)

Index

Macdonald & Evans Ltd. publish a wide range
of titles on Dance and Movement and related subjects
A selection of these are described on the
following pages.

For a full list of titles and prices write for the
FREE Dance and Movement leaflet available from:
Department BP1, Macdonald & Evans Ltd., Estover,
Plymouth PL6 7PZ